Eliot McCormick, und Andere

Wonder Stories of Travel

Eliot McCormick, und Andere

Wonder Stories of Travel

ISBN/EAN: 9783337210083

Printed in Europe, USA, Canada, Australia, Japan

Cover: Foto ©Andreas Hilbeck / pixelio.de

More available books at **www.hansebooks.com**

"I ACTUALLY FELL ASLEEP."

OF
TRAVEL

BY

ELIOT McCORMICK, ERNEST INGERSOLL,
E. E. BROWN, DAVID KER,
AND OTHERS

Illustrated

BOSTON
D. LOTHROP AND COMPANY
32 Franklin Street

ERAL GRANT AT EPHESUS.

THE Turkish battery ashore thundered a royal salute to General Grant as the *Vandalia* which bore him from port to port in the Mediterranean steamed up to her anchorage in the harbor of Smyrna. Thirty great iron-clads followed in quick succession; men-of-war crowded the harbor. They had been ordered into Turkish waters on account of the war then raging between Turkey and Russia. From ship and shore thousands of spectators watched the *Vandalia's* approach with eager interest, and from the foremast of every vessel and the flagstaffs of the city the American flag waved the General a glad and hearty welcome.

No one in all the city was more pleased at his arrival than Fred Martin, the son of an American merchant resident in Smyrna. He stood with the crowd upon the quay cheering enthusiastically.

Fred had sailed with his mother from New York when he was but three years old, and his memories of his native land were consequently vague and fanciful. His playmates were the little Greek and Armenian boys of his neighborhood, and the few English children belonging to the British consulate. He had told his comrades, in glowing words, the history of General Grant. Fred was very precocious, and had learned several languages. In his play with the Greek boys he had learned to speak Greek, and in the same pleasant way the Armenian boys had taught him their language. Besides, in the streets and bazaars he had picked up Turkish and Arabic enough to converse quite easily with the merchants speaking those languages. So great was Fred's proficiency that at home he went by the name of "the little polyglot."

The boys shouted and cheered till they found that General Grant would not come ashore that day, and gradually they departed for their homes. We will leave General Grant to receive the official courtesies

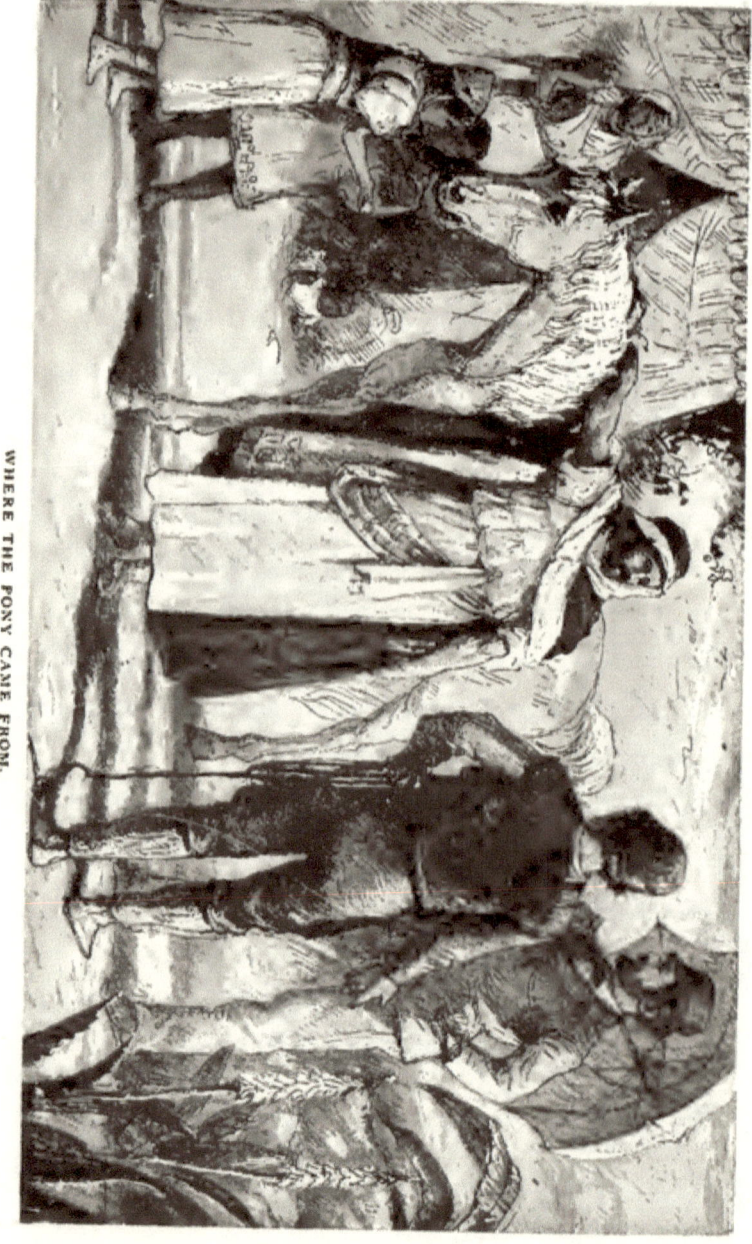

WHERE THE PONY CAME FROM.

of the authorities of the city and the admirals and captains of the fleet, and proceed with Master Fred.

Fred was the owner of a beautiful little Arabian horse, which made him the envy of every boy of his acquaintance. This horse was the Christmas gift of his father. Christmas eve he had been secretly led to Mr. Martin's stable, that in the morning Fred might receive a happy surprise. Early Christmas morning Fred was sent to the stable on some trifling errand, and what was his astonishment to see a new horse quietly munching his breakfast. His delight knew no bounds when he found a blue ribbon tied around the pony's neck (for Fred at once called him a pony), to which was attached a card, on which was written :

"Fred Martin. From his affectionate father, Christmas, 1877."

The pony had been purchased from an Arab. This Arab with his little family had wandered far from his own country, and at length had settled in the environs of Smyrna. Through sickness and poverty he was compelled to part with his beautiful horse, his children crying bitterly, and fondly caressing him, as he was led away from the tent.

Mr. Martin's conscience almost smote him as he witnessed this poor family's grief; but the Arab motioned to him to hasten away, signifying that the children would soon forget their sorrow.

The pony, as he was called, was of the purest Arabian blood. He was so gentle that Fred's little sisters ran into his stall and played without hesitation around his feet. Yet he had all the metal and fire of his royal race. In color he was milk-white, and his neck arched like the curve of an ivory bow. His head was small and elegant; so perfect, indeed, that an artist had taken it as a model for a handsome ideal Arabian in a fine picture he was painting. The pony's ears were satin-like, and responded to the slightest impression with a quick, tremulous movement that betokened the keenest intelligence. His eyes beamed with affection and loyalty. Ladies delighted to run their fingers through his soft, silken hair; and they loved to pet him as he held his nose to them to be stroked, as they would a beautiful child.

Fred had read the lives of Alexander the Great and Sir Walter Scott. He had been charmed by the allusions to their fondness for riding and hunting in their boyhood days, and he emulated them in many a gallop and chase among the hills surrounding the city. Many a hare and partridge had he run down and shot, and brought home in triumph hanging to the pommel of his saddle. Many a time he had startled the shepherds and frightened their sheep by dashing upon them around some sharp curve, for which misdemeanor he had to put spurs to the pony to escape the shepherds' wrath. Besides, he had ridden to many places which travellers go thousands of miles to see. He could point out the different layers in the walls of the old castle overlooking the city, which was first built by Alexander the Great, and last by the Saracens. He could guide travellers to the beautiful ruins of an ancient temple erected to Homer; and several times he had ridden into the very cave where many scholars believe the great poet Homer at one time lived. These excursions were attended by many dangers, but somehow Fred came out of them unharmed.

After General Grant had been several days in

Smyrna, Fred was overjoyed at receiving an invitation to accompany him on a grand excursion to the ruined city of Ephesus, lying fifty miles from Smyrna. His father told him that he might take the pony with him, as several freight-cars were to be filled with horses and donkeys for the use of the party. The Pasha — the governor of that district of Turkey — had arranged for this excursion as his greatest compliment to General Grant. He chartered a large train; ordered a mounted body-guard of Turkish officers to proceed to Ephesus, and a regiment of troops to receive the General at the depot with military honors. The party needed a strong military escort, for at Ephesus there are robbers who live in caves, and watch for distinguished visitors, whom they sometimes capture, and demand a heavy ransom for their release.

Fred galloped early to the depot. He kept the pony quiet amid the general confusion, with extreme difficulty. The donkey drivers were mercilessly pounding the donkeys, and yelling at them, to get them into the car; the grooms were struggling with the restive horses; dogs were yelping; the soldiers were going through their exercises, and there was a bewildering medley of unpleasant sounds.

By much persistence Fred got the pony into a car with a fine gray horse and a snow-white mule sent from the Pasha's stables for General and Mrs. Grant. Fred was almost wonder-struck at the sight of these beautiful animals. The horse was dressed in gorgeous housings. The saddle was heavily embroidered and plated with gold ; even the buckles and rings were of gold, and a rich gold filigree work covered the bridle and portions of the reins and girths. Fred had heard of the richness of Oriental accoutrements, but he was not prepared for such magnificence as this. The mule was not dressed so regally, but being regarded a sacred animal by the Pasha, a queen could not have desired a greater compliment than was offered Mrs. Grant in the sending of this mule for her use.

When the General arrived, all things were ready, and the train swept out into an enchanting valley. Past Turkish villages it ran, the little Turkish boys, like many boys in more civilized countries, giving it a vigorous salute with pebbles as it hurried on. Often it passed trains of camels making their tedious way to bordering countries, and occasionally a hunter and his dogs would seem to start out of a jungle or hillside, as if on purpose to delight Master Fred.

In an hour's time the train thundered over the river Cayster and shot into the depot at Ayasolook. Instantly all was confusion again. The horses and donkeys were hustled out of the cars. The horses were arranged in cavalry line, and the donkeys were drawn up in the rear. General Grant gave the signal to mount, and the men of the party instantly vaulted into the saddle. The white mule had been behaving strangely for an animal of his reputation, and Mrs. Grant was advised not to undertake to ride him. She wisely listened to advice, for the mule turned out on this particular occasion to be very careless with his heels, and to have a very abrupt way of stopping, which obliged his rider to travel on a short distance alone. Mrs. Grant had been so well acquainted with mules in the West that she had in fact no confidence even in a sacred mule. By some means she with the other ladies got the smallest and most tired-looking donkeys. Now they put spurs to their horses, leaving the donkeys with their unfortunate riders far behind.

For a moment only they stop to look at the few pieces of glittering marble which are all that remain of the snowy blocks and columns of the once glorious temple of Diana. They decide to skirt the plain lying between Ayasolook and Ephesus, by riding along an ancient breakwater; they pause for an instant to listen to the rustle of the long grass against the wall where once was heard the ebb and flow of the sea. Up they climb among a whole cluster of temples, stopping only to look at the face of a shattered statue, or at a beautiful carved hand extended almost beseechingly from a heap of rubbish. The horses stumble through public squares, regaining solid footing for an instant on some broad pedestal of a once world-renowned monument. Now Fred's pony flounders in the basin of an old fountain, into which he has been forced to leap. The ruins seem to rise up in waves, and they are obliged to dismount and lead their horses up to the great theatre, where they halt for rest and lunch.

Fred tied the pony to the foot of a prostrate Apollo and slipped away to explore this great building for himself. He climbed to the top of the hill, on the side of which the theatre was built, and looked in wonder upon the stage far below. This great interior contained seats for 50,000 people. Fred fancied he could almost hear the thunder of applause from distant ages, like the far-away roar of the sea. He now clambered down to look at the foundations of the building. The great pillars and arches stood as firmly as the day on which they were completed. St. Paul had looked upon the same grand architecture that he now beheld.

As he looked he began to stir the earth carelessly with his whip-handle. Suddenly he brought a curious object to the surface, which he picked up and carefully examined. With his knife he dug away the erosion, and saw by the glitter underneath that the object was of gold. In other places something which he could not cut resisted his knife. It now occurred to him that he had found a bracelet, and he hastened to the company with his treasure. An antiquarian in the party, upon close examination, found that Fred had unearthed what had been a very costly bracelet. It was of rare design, and set all around with precious stones; doubtless it had glittered many times upon the fair arm of some ancient performer. All were delighted at Fred's discovery, and felt that this little *souvenir* in itself would make the day memorable. In a short time they had visited the market-place, the stadium — a building which held 76,000 people — the odeon, or music hall, and the cave of the Seven Sleepers, and were ready to start back.

As several conjectured, on their return General Grant proposed a grand race. Lying between them and the depot was a smooth plain three miles in extent. On the further side a leaning column could be seen, which was at once selected as the reaching-post. A Turkish officer was chosen umpire and sent on in advance. General Grant had noticed Fred's pony many times during the day, and was greatly pleased with his exquisite beauty. He thought it possible that the pony might be the sharpest competitor his own elegant, high-spirited gray would have in the race, and he beckoned Fred to take a position at his side. The starting-point was to be an immense sarcophagus, in which a noble Greek had once been buried, but which now, from some cause, lay upturned on the edge of the plain. At this place ten superbly mounted horsemen drew up in line, with General Grant and Fred on the right.

The English consul gave the signal for starting.

Fred shook the reins upon the pony's neck, and he bounded forward as gracefully as a deer. The pony instinctively prepared himself for the race. Both horses were of princely pedigree and showed their blood in the sylph-like ease with which they moved. Fred knew that in horsemanship the odds must be greatly in favor of General Grant. How Fred admired him as he sat upon the gray, every inch the general; and he felt almost alarmed at the thought of contesting the race with such a splendid horseman! But he quickly made up his mind to compete for the honors as sharply as he could. His light weight he knew to be in his favor, and he had all confidence in the pony's speed and courage; even then he could feel him tremble under his growing excitement.

They all had made an even start, and for many rods had kept together; but now Fred and the General began to push ahead. The pony's silken tail brushed the shoulder of the foremost horse, while his

NEITHER THE GENERAL NOR FRED SEEMED TO GAIN AN INCH!

handsome mane tossed against the bridle-rein of his antagonist.

It was a fine sight to see these two beautiful horses settle down for the remaining two-mile run. The movement of each was perfect. There was no convulsive effort, no waste of energy. They glided onward as smoothly as the flight of birds. Nose to nose, neck to neck, shoulder to shoulder they flew. Neither the General nor Fred seemed to gain an inch, and neither seemed to care whether the other won or not. Patches of meadow grass brilliant with wild flowers, pieces of rich sculpture, a thousand rare objects that once shone in beautiful houses or more beautiful temples, lay scattered along their course; but they were unnoticed in the glorious speed.

But a half-mile remains, and each horse is making his best time. The sun lights up horses and riders, so that they seem like phantoms sweeping over the plain. Now with a bound they cross a wide ditch, the General's horse distancing the pony by several feet. The pony clings to him like a shadow. One touch of the spur upon his hot flank, and he recovers his lost ground. Never was there so close a race before! Now it is whip and spur, words of command and words of encouragement, and the horses seem scarcely to touch the ground. Now the General leads, now Fred. The goal is reached!

The umpire did not decide.

Fred told the Greek boy that night that he won it. If you are anxious to know who did win, ask the General.

INDIAN CHILDREN AND THEIR PETS.

MANY people suppose that the Indian children have no dolls or pets.

This is a mistake. The Indian baby, or pappoose, is provided by its squaw-mother with a sort of doll from its earliest infancy.

The baby itself is tied to a board which is covered with buckskins and fanciful bindings, or with bright-colored cloth ornamented with bead-work and tinsel. This baby-board, which is carriage and cradle in one, looks like the toe of a large slipper, and has a piece of wood bent across the head to protect its little copper-colored occupant from being struck by anything. Just as her convenience may prompt, the squaw hangs her pappoose, thus cradled, on her back while walking, or in a tree when working about the tent, or on

INDIAN CHILDREN AND THEIR PETS.

the saddle pommel as represented in the picture. From the protecting headboard hangs suspended the doll composed of feathers, beads and red cloth, per-

LITTLE INDIAN GIRLS AND THEIR "PAPPOOSES."

haps representing an Indian warrior. The little pappoose looks at this dangling image all day long, and this monotonous endeavor often causes a horrible squint from which the little Indian never recovers.

The squaw-mothers sometimes make miniature pappooses, bound to cradle-boards in fancy covering, like their own, for the older children to play with; but it is a still commoner sight to see the girls carrying a puppy in a little blanket over their shoulders. It seems strange that they should make of their pets what is considered the greatest delicacy, puppy-stew, which is the chief dish of a feast given in commemoration of a child having become a certain age.

The little Indians also make pets of crows. A little girl will often daily carry about with her a wicker basket filled with baby crows just as they are taken from the nest by her brother. Beside her an old dog will often be wiled along, dragging her puppies in a similar net or basket stretched across transverse poles.

The Indian boys have pet colts to ride; and they make pets of young eagles, which they put on a sort of stand with a string attached to one leg to prevent the birds from flying away.

The boys also early learn to use the bow and

arrows, and are often occupied in driving blackbirds and cowbirds from the growing maize.

Corn is the only vegetable cultivated by the Indian, and the Chippewas, who are semi-civilized, grind

LITTLE INDIAN GIRLS AND THEIR PETS.

their corn into a sort of coarse samp by pounding it in a mortar with a wooden pestle. They also roast the ears, and dry it for winter use. Great groups of children will sit with a squaw (perhaps mending moccasins) to help them at their work and preserve order, on high platforms the whole day, overlooking the

AN "INDIAN MEAL."

corn-fields, so as to drive away the birds as they alight in flocks. Picture No. 3 represents a group at a little "Indian meal," which plays both ways — as it is Indian meal they are feasting on. The lodges, or tepees, in the background are peculiar to the Chippewa tribe, being made of birch bark wrapped around poles.

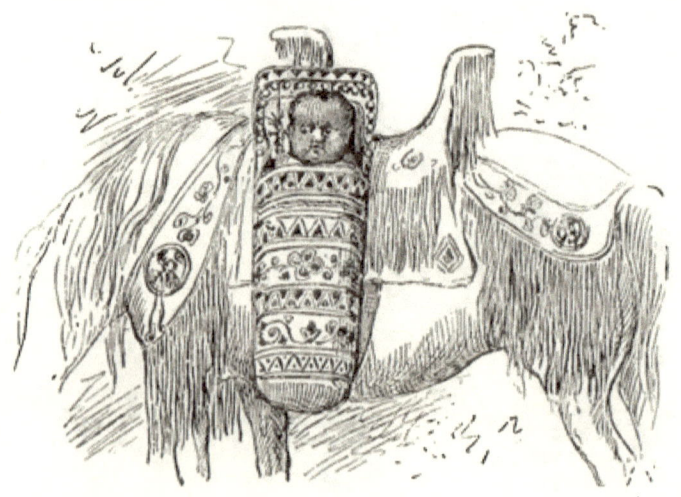

INDIAN BABY AND DOLL.

The older boys amuse themselves by different games while tending the horses, one of which is represented. First they spread upon the ground a buffalo hide on which they kneel facing each other.

Then one takes a little stick and passes it from one hand to the other, first behind and then before, while the other boy guesses which hand it is in. He is entitled to three guesses. The first, if right, counts him three; the second, two; and the third, one. If he misses altogether, he loses according to the number put up for stake. The one guessing designates his guess by hitting his right or left shoulder, according to the hand he thinks his opponent holds it in.

This, like all other Indian games, is made interesting by the stakes, which generally consist of some ornament, or some service to be rendered.

"WHICH, RIGHT OR LEFT?"

RIGA IN THE CHIMNEY.

HOW did Riga get into the chimney?
Well, if the truth must be told, it was not merely a chimney, but the window; and not a window only, but the front door; and not only the front door, but the staircase. It was, in fact, so much of all four, that it was but slightly like any one of them. Things were altogether upside-down in this house. Instead of being built on the ground like all reasonable houses, it was under it; and although it had but one place to come in at, and but one fire to cook at, so many people lived inside of it in tents of their own that it was in reality a village; and yet again, it was a village where you had only to lift the skin wall of your one-roomed dwelling to get into your neighbor's.

The land was Kamschatka, and Riga was a small

boy of that cold country. He had been outside to get some milk from the deer, and had come to the hole that formed the entrance, and taken the first step down on the notched pole that was to land him in the fire if he didn't take a good leap over when he got to the bottom.

It was already dark. Above him one of the dogs — there were twenty or thirty in all — got a smell of the milk, or a smell of a pot on the fire; and as he sniffed greedily through chimney (we might as well call it that), he lost his balance and came tumbling head and heels over Riga with a prodigious racket and howling into the village below. Riga, who was fat, thought he was going too; but he clung to the notched pole till he had his senses again, and then he clung the tighter because of something else.

At the foot of the pole burned a fire of moss which gave much heat, little light, and more smoke than anything else; this smoke hung duskily around the chimney, and went out lazily as it happened to feel inclined. Riga's entrance had been covered by the dog's fall, the smoke and dust hid him effectually, and something stopped him from coming down. It was a little whisper which, although addressed to a person close by the whisperer's side, scaled the pole for the benefit of Riga's curious ears.

"Hush! some one came in."

"You are mistaken, for no one comes down."

"Some one is listening, then."

"Lopka, you suspect everything. Who would stop up there, and why? and who would know there was anything to listen to?"

Riga was listening, however; and although his position was most uncomfortable, his curiosity was so excited by hearing a conversation which was not intended for any one to hear, that he bent his ears more eagerly than ever, and was as silent as a snowflake.

"When can it be done?" whispered Lopka shrilly.

"When all are asleep."

"We may be asleep too."

"Trust me for that."

"Can we get out without rousing the sleepers? Do you think the herd will be quiet?"

"We have no one to fear but the curious Riga; that boy always has one ear open."

"That is so;" thought Riga in the chimney, "and now I see the wisdom of it." He gave a movement of satisfaction, and some of the milk splashed hissing down into the fire.

"What is that, Svorovitch?" asked Lopka.

"I have often heard that sound in the fire," was the reply, "and my father says if it is a saint's day, the saint weeps for some wrong done."

At this moment the thick pungent smoke tickled Riga's nose, and he gave vent to three good hearty sneezes. The two boys below jumped to their feet and ran away.

"There is still more, and it may be learned by listening," murmured Riga as he went down. "I am not a saint, but I will do more than weep if any wrong is about to be done."

It was the winter time; the cold was intense. If you should put your uncovered face out of doors, the eyelashes would freeze to your cheeks. The weather was so fierce, the clouds so threatening, that but few of the men had ventured out; such as had, rode up swiftly on their sledges at nightfall, set the deer free among the herd, and gathered round the fire to sleep, or talk over the adventures of the day.

Among other things, this bitterest night of all, they returned to the conversation of several preceding nights, about two Englishmen with their guide, belated by the snows of an early winter. These travellers had pressed on towards a port on the coast, thinking to winter there comfortably until some ship would sail for San Francisco; but reports had now reached the tribe of a fatal accident to one of the reindeer; and wise Lodovin shook his head. He was seventy years old, and knew everything.

"There was a spot," he said, "near the Kamschatkan shore, a hut underground constructed from a wrecked vessel by some sailors. All guides know of this place. There was fuel there, and they would not freeze; but they could have had no provisions worth speaking of, and either they must die of starvation, or go on and perish in the coming storm upon the toondra."

This had been repeated each night since Lodovin had heard of the dead deer; but his listeners were willing to receive an observation many times for want of fresher.

Usually Riga sat long in the midst of the circle; but to-night he withdrew early to his particular home, a small enclosure a few feet square, where the whole family slept, lighted by a bit of moss floating in oil. He had seen Lopka enter the next room; and the fear of missing him brought him early to lie on his own floor where he could peep beneath the edge of the skin. Later, when everything was quiet, the same anxiety made him crawl out and take up his old place on the notched pole, where he clung silent and immovable, but listening and looking intently, every sense merged into his sense of curiosity.

Ah, woe to Riga in the chimney! two quiet figures suddenly came straight to the pole, and one began to mount. To mount? Yes; and seeing Riga, to seize him by the foot and sternly bid him be silent and go out.

In spite of his sturdy saintship, the surprised Riga was frightened to death by the knife in Svorovitch's hand; and not daring to disobey, he tremblingly did as he was told.

He was speedily followed by Lopka and Svorovitch. Holding him well, and forcing him to assist them, the youths fastened to a sled three of the best and fleetest deer of the herd, which Riga very well knew did not belong to them. That done, they paid no attention to his entreaties, but taking him with them in the sled, the long, steady pace of the deer soon left their home behind them.

Riga now began to cry and beg them to spare his life. "You are going to cut my throat and bury me in the toondra," he said. "You had better not, or I will do you some harm as soon as I am a saint."

Svorovitch burst into a loud laugh. "Cut your throat!" he said; "child, the tempest and the cold may kill you, but we shan't. No, you might be safe this minute if we could have trusted you to go back and be quiet. But we know you would have waked the whole tribe to ask questions of what we were about, and they would have followed us."

From what Lopka and Svorovitch spoke of after this, Riga learned they were bound on a journey to some distant point and were racing to reach it against the storm. Further than that he learned nothing, for he was too sleepy now to be inquisitive, and, carefully sheltered by his companions, he soon lost all consciousness of even his own fat little person.

An Arctic winter storm on the great toondra — do you know what that means? Fancy three of the worst snow-storms that ever you have seen, taking place at one and the same time, the fierce, icy bitter wind roaring and sweeping with terrible force across an endless plain, the air blinding, sight impossible, and you will know why Lopka and Svorovitch, and even Riga, gazed often and anxiously at the clouds throughout the following day. With eyes and ears always on the alert, and well on the alert at that, our little saint thought he heard now and then strange sounds of great distant winds nearing them, and at last he began to discover, as he peered upwards, the thick look in the air that tells that snow is on the way.

"The wind is rising," said Riga. "You ought to take me home;" but though he wished to cry, he kept his tears back bravely. Suddenly he cried out, "The storm!"

And it was the storm, the great Arctic storm, coming all at once, blinding and thick, borne on the wind, and sweeping over the ground as if it never meant to stop or rest there.

"We can go no further," cried Svorovitch. "We, too, shall be lost!"

"Don't despair, little brother," said Lopka, but at the same time turning away his face.

Here the alert little Riga lifted his fat face to tell them that he had for some time heard the ocean, and that just as the snow appeared he had seen a volcano in the ground; perhaps from these signs they could tell where they were.

The roaring of the tempest was so terrible that it was now impossible to distinguish the sound of the waves; but when Riga was questioned as to his volcano, and could only answer that he had seen smoke coming directly from the ground in a certain direction, Svorovitch exclaimed aloud, and springing out of the sledge ran a few feet from them. Following the sound of his voice, Riga and Lopka found him on his knees with his head bent above a black pipe setting a little above the earth.

"They are here," he cried, "it is the place! They answer me."

In a few moments the figure of a man appeared in the storm, seized upon them, and leading them a few steps further, descended by a slanting passage into a snug little under-ground cabin, free of smoke and passably light, where the boys found themselves face to face with the two English travellers. Their mutual explanations, though given with some difficulty, showed how the guide had stolen off with the remaining deer and left them to their fate, and that that morning they had eaten the last of their provisions; and how the adventurous Lopka and Svorovitch, pitying their condition, had determined to set out and save them at any risk. Riga comprehended what was not explained to the Englishmen — that it was undertaken in secret, for neither of the boys yet owned deer of their own, and had no hope of being successful in borrowing such as they needed. After all, he had not guessed rightly in the chimney, and he felt that there is something more to know of people than what one finds out by eavesdropping. Things half heard often look wrong: when the whole is seen they may turn out nobly right.

The gratitude of the travellers to the brave young Kamschatkans was great; and although the food they had brought was only dried fish, and some fat of the whale, it was the best they had, and a heartier and happier supper was seldom eaten. The storm continued throughout that night; but clearing off the next morning, the party were able to start on their return journey to the village. The deer, who know their masters, and will seldom desert the place where they are, were ready to return, and carried them back at a pace which, although not as fleet as that of a horse, was more unflagging and reliable. Welcome from all parties greeted their arrival, no harsh words met them; the parents were only too glad to have their brave boys safe again, the owners of the deer too happy that their property was restored unhurt. Only the wise Lodovin shook his head.

"If the boys begin like that," said he, "what do you suppose the men will do? Take care how you praise those who respect no man's property!" For Lodovin owned one of the deer which the boys had borrowed. As for fat little Riga, he had gained so much glory (you must remember it was he who had discovered the smoke-pipe) by hanging in the chimney, that it became his favorite position, to the everlasting danger of the limbs of the tribe and his own head, and also to the great confusion of such unwary beings as weekly told secrets about the village fire.

THE POPE'S GUARD.

SEEING THE POPE.

IT is only the young people of America who, in this age of the world, have not been to Europe; therefore to them and for them I have written down, in journal form, a few incidents of travel; among them, a brief account of an evening spent with La Baronessa Von Stein, and a presentation to the Pope.

Wednesday. This evening we have spent, by invitation, with the Baroness Von Stein, widow of Baron Von Stein of Germany. The Baroness, a German by birth, passed much of her youth in Poland. Skilled as a horsewoman, she often joined her father in rural pastimes, shooting, hunting etc. Being perfectly well, and of great mind, she acquired, as do all the noble women of Europe, a thorough knowledge of the ancient classics in their originals; also a familiarity with nearly every spoken language of the Old and New World. Well comparing with Margaret, Queen of Navarre in fluency of tongue, she readily changes from Italian to French, from French to Spanish quotes from Buckle, Draper, etc., in English, is quite at home on German philosophy, notwithstanding her devotion to the Catholic Church. A singularly attractive old lady is she now; rather masculine in manner, exceedingly so, in mind; a fine painter in oil to whom the Pope has sat, in person, for his portrait. We have seen the likeness. It is pronounced perfect. She is very anxious for us to see his Holiness, and we certainly shall not leave Rome without so doing. The Baroness has an autograph note from Pio Nono, which is a rare possession. This she displayed with far more pride than was apparent upon showing her own handiwork. When the Holy Father sat to her, in order to get the true expression, conversation was necessary and she repeated, with much satisfaction, snatches therefrom, which were of the brightest nature. However learned *he* may be, in the Baroness Von Stein he meets no inferior.

As we entered her room, she was smoking: she begged pardon, but continued the performance.

The cigar was a cigar, no cigarette, no white-coated article, but a long, large, brown Havana, such as gentlemen in our own country use.

"You will find no difficulty," said she, between her

whiffs, "in seeing 'Il Papa,' and then you will say how good is his picture."

During a part of our interview, there was present a sister of a "Secretaris Generalissmoi to the Pope," who told us the manner in which the Popeship will be filled—she talked only in Italian, but I give a literal translation. "The new Pope is approved by the present Pio Nono. His name is written upon paper by the present Pope and sealed. The document is seen by no one, till after the death of 'Il Papa,' when it is opened, as a will, by the proper power. Unlike a will, it can not be disputed."

Pio Nono certainly had his election in a far different way, according to the statements of the Roman Exiles of that day.

As the life of his Majesty hangs upon eternity, the matter of a successor will soon be decided. "Antonelli gone, where will it fall!" said I, but at once perceived that I was trespassing and the subject was speedily changed.

We left the Baronessa, intent upon one thing, viz., a presentation to the Pope, as soon as practical. Our Consul being no longer accredited to this power, but to Victor Emanuel, we must apply elsewhere.

Thursday. Started early this morning, from my residence corner of Bacca di Leone and Bia di Lapa (doubtful protectors), for the American College and Father Chatard, in order to get a "permit" to the Monday Reception at the Vatican. On my way (and those who know Rome as well as we do will know how much on the way) I took, as I do upon all occasions, the Roman and Trajan forums, always walking when practicable; by the above means, I am likely to become very familiar with these beautiful views. They are so fascinating that I can not begin any day's work without taking these first. The Trajan is my favorite. It may not be uninteresting to mention here that, on my circuitous stroll to the said College, I saw, and halted the better to see, one of those picturesque groups of Contadini and Contadine who frequent the towns of Italy. There were, first the parents, dressed in the fantastic garb of their class of peasantry, i. e., the mother with the long double pads, one scarlet and one white, hanging over her head and neck, while the father wore a gay slouched hat; then three girls, severally garbed in short pink dress, blue apron embroidered with every conceivable color, simple and combined, yellow handkerchief thrown over the chest, long earrings, heavy braids, bare-footed or in fancifully knit shoes.

Two boys in equally remarkable attire, and a baby that looked like a butterfly, completed the domestic

ROMAN CONTADINA.

circle. They did not seem to mind my gaze. The father continued his smoking, the mother her knitting, the girls their hooking, the boys their listless lounging, and the baby its play in the dust. There was a charm in the scene. One sight however (to be sure mine was an extended opportunity) is sufficient. A few steps beyond this gathering, I found photographs colored to represent these vagrants, and at one store pictures of the very individuals — I purchased specimens to take to America, a novelty the other side of the Atlantic.

After an hour or two, I reached the American College, was met by the students who very politely directed me to the Concièrge, and my name was taken to the learned Father. The students all wore the long robe, though speaking English.

Being a Quaker by birth, therefore educated to respect every man's religion, and to believe that every man respects mine, nevertheless I felt misgivings incumbent upon the meeting of extremes. I was ushered into a large drawing-room and was examining the pictures, which generally tell the character of the owner, when Mr. Chatard entered. As he asked me to be seated, I thought, as some one has expressed it before me, "the whole world over, there are but two kinds of people, — 'man and woman.'"

The youth of this college may thank their stars that America has given them one of her most learned and worthy sons, though the sect to which his mother once belonged must deplore his loss.

In conversation with this Reverend gentleman, I obtained the requirements necessary to an introduction to the Pope, and was a little surprised that he should question my willingness to conform to the same. It was however, explained. He had been much embarrassed by the demeanor of some of the American women. Seeking the privilege of meeting the Pope in his own palace, where common courtesy and etiquette naturally demand a deference to the Lord of the Manor, yet these ladies, having previously guaranteed a compliance with the laws of ceremony, after gaining admission refused to obey them.

Seeing the Pope was not, to me, a religious service and is not generally so considered.

My only fear was that my plain manners in their brusqueness, would have the appearance of "omission."

But the requirements are simple. Bending the knee, as a physical performance, was a source of anxiety. I at once called to mind the great difficulty which, as a young girl, I had in the play:

> "If I *had* as many wives
> As the stars in the skies," etc.

Notwithstanding the person who had to kneel in the game had a large cushion to throw before her to receive the fall, I always shook the house from the foundations when I went down. I can hear the pendants now, of a chandelier in a certain frame house in my native town ring out my weight, as I flung the cushion in front of a boy that knew " he was not the one," and took to my knees. True, the Vatican is not shaky in its underpinnnings, and faithful practice upon the floor of my apartment in Bocca di Leone, I thought, would be productive of some good. Quickly running through this train of reflection, and finally trusting that the gathering would not be disturbed by any marked awkwardness, I returned home to await the tidings.

Monday Evening. Have seen Pio Nono — have committed no enormity.

According to directions, in black dress, black veil, *à la* Spanish lady, ungloved hands (what an appearance at a Presidential reception!) we were attired. Took a carriage for the Vatican. Before we left home the padrona viewed us, pronounced us all right, and earnestly sought the privilege of selecting a coach for us. She had an eye to style. Is it possible that she did not give us credit for the same "strength," and we traveling Americans? It is to be confessed that the horses were less like donkeys than otherwise might have been. Trying the knee the last thing before leaving the house, there was certainly reason for encouragement, though still a lingering humility.

Our ride was subdued, but we reached St. Peter's, passed through the elegant halls of the Pope's Palace, surpassed only by those of the Pitti at Florence in their gold and fresco, and were ushered into the reception room of Pio Nono.

This apartment, long and narrow, seemed more like a corridor than a hall. Its beauties are described in various guide books, so that "they who read can see."

We were the only Protestants. The other ladies were laden with magnificent rosaries, pictures, toys, ribbons, etc., for the Holy Father's blessing. Even I purchased one of the first, viz., a rosary, to undergo the same ceremony, as a gift to a much-loved servant girl at home.

We sat here many minutes in quiet (inwardly longing to try the fall.) At length the Pope was led in. We forgot our trials. A countenance so benign, beaming with goodness, spread a cheer throughout the assembly. We took the floor naturally and involuntarily. Except in dress, he might have been any old patriarch. The white robe, long and plain, gave him rather the appearance of a matriarch.

It chanced that his Holiness passed first up the right side of the hall. We sat *vis à vis*, so that we had the benefit of all that he said before we came in turn. While addressing the right, who continue on their knees, the left rise. As he turns to the latter they again kneel, whereas those opposite change from this posture to the standing.

The Pope talked now in French, now in Italian, mostly in the former. As he approached our party, we were introduced merely as Americans, but our religion was stamped upon our brows. Turning kindly to my young daughter, who wore, as an ornament, a chain and cross, he said, as if quite sure of the fact, " *You* can wear your cross outside, as an adornment; I am obliged to wear mine inside as a cross;" whereupon, with a smile, he drew this emblem from his wide ribbon sash, showing her a most elegant massive cross of gold and diamonds, probably the most valuable one in the world. As he replaced this mark of his devotion, his countenance expressing a recognition of our Protestantism, perhaps a pity for our future, placing his hand upon our heads, he passed on. The blessing of a good old man, whatever his faith, can injure no one, and may not be without its efficacy, even though it rest upon a disciple of George Fox.

I shall never cease to be glad that I have seen Pio Nono.

A LESSON IN ITALIAN.

"Do you speak English?"
"*Non, Signora!*"
"Do you speak any other language than Italian?"
"*Non, Signora!*"
"Then you are the person I desire as guide!"

The above dialogue took place near the Amphitheatre of Verona. The Italian, standing awaiting employment, was an old man, bright and active. The American, who addressed him was an elderly woman, who had studied the languages of Europe nearly half a century. She had just arrived in Verona. Leaving the younger members of her party she had strolled off alone, the better, as she said, to air her lore. One must be alone to succeed with a foreign tongue; an audience of one's own countrymen is particularly distracting if not embarrassing.

Following her leader into the Amphitheatre she

sat where, ages ago, the Royalty had done, and commenced audible reflections to this effect:

"Did scenes such as took place here have a charm for court ladies, ladies educated as were the Zenobias and the Julias of those days?"

She had no idea that her language could be understood, but the guide vociferated as if angry:

"People of those days were great, strong, just!"

She felt that she was answered, but nevertheless was practicing her Italian.

The Amphitheatre of Verona, being in a state of preservation, is a good introduction to the Coliseum at Rome. The old man, my guide, was present at the Congress of 1822, when twenty-two thousand persons were seated within its walls. The Chariot Entrance is pointed out, also that through which the culprits came ; and the gate which held back the hungry animal longing for his prize. These oft told tales were recited by the guide, as are the speeches of Daniel Webster by the American school-boy, learned and rehearsed many times, till the traveler, having exhausted her own vocabulary as applied to this show, seemed ready to depart.

"Cathedrals," proposed the conductor as a matter of course. Cathedrals consequently obtained.

In one of these of the time of Charlemagne, the guide

seized with a religious zeal, begged his companion to be seated while he joined in the services. She could not conscientiously interfere with his soul's instincts, therefore consented to rest awhile.

The performances seemed exceedingly tedious, as the monotone of the priest was relieved only by the click of the collections. But the old man was very devout, never allowing the box to pass without his contribution. Magnanimous spirit! How many of our home churches would give twice and thrice without wincing?

Growing rather anxious to leave these premises, the Protestant tried to hurry the brother-at-prayer by a motion towards the door.

"Will Madame condescend a ten minutes longer? A collection for a deceased infant is next."

Madame did condescend. The coin was deposited. After this emotional act the twain left the church, the guide very gay and lively, the lady rather moved to compassion. Suppose her companion *were* steeped in ignorance, how beautiful his faith!

"Was the little child a relative, or were its parents his friends?"

"Oh, no! he had never heard of it in life, but only a hard heart would keep one so young and alone in the shades." Here he wiped a tear.

A Lesson in Italian.

The guide turned, quickly melting into the smile again, remarking: "The Tombs of the Scaligers.

These monuments are indeed worth seeing, especially that of the last of this great family. This Scaliger, to outdo his ancestry had spent many years laboring with his own hands upon the marble which was to mark his resting-place. The devices were his own; no other person was employed in the hewing, the cutting, even in the erection of this showy memorial. Its maker died satisfied with the result of his lifetime, a work for ages to succeed.

The oldest of this name rests under a comparatively simple canopy. During the First Napoleon's time this tomb was opened that a cast might be made of the head, there being no authentic representation extant; and by order of the Emperor, the bust was placed in the Louvre at Paris, and sketches of this wonderfully fine head sold for great sums.

"The house of the Capulets," said the old man.

Standing beneath the balcony on the very spot where stood poor Romeo (or Charlotte Cushman as well), quite absorbed in the few lines of Shakspeare that floated in her mind, the lady was aroused from her revery by the guide, who, pointing at the almost obliterated coat-of-arms, said ambitiously:

"*Chapeau, capello, Inglese!*"

A Lesson in Italian.

At the same time he crushed his head-gear, till his face was quite covered.

"Hat!" shrieked she, judging that one who can not speak English must be deaf to this tongue though in proper condition to hear his native. If there is any letter that an Italian cannot pronounce, it is the "h." His attempts were many and fruitless. At length, violently coughing out the aspirate, he added with great gusto the "at" and was satisfied though exhausted. His next effort was "how;" his next "head," and finally "woman." If there is any letter after "h" that the Italian can *not* get, it is our "w" and lo! his choice of first steps in English, "hat, head, how and woman."

Passing through the market-places which are gorgeous in the distance, but whose goods when inspected are very common, they were met by many beggars. To those dressed in a peculiar garb the guide invariably gave, at no time to those in any other suit. He always reached the mite with a smile, good soul that he was!

Overlooking the lovely Adige they stood upon the great bridge, when it suddenly occurred to madame that the humble individual beside her might be giving her more time than customary, even as he had freely given to God's "poor in other respects."

A Lesson in Italian.

Feeling satisfied with her day's work and knowing her way to the hotel, she commenced the process of bidding him adieu — in more common parlance, "getting clear of him."

"I am indeed obliged to you," began she. "I have learned so much Ital—"

Here she was interrupted by the sage Mentor.

"If madame is so well pleased with my services, as she has taught me much English (the hypocrite,) I shall take but *twelve lire.*"

"*Twelve lire!*" she quietly repeated after him, while her astonishment was mingling with rage within, so as to render her voice almost inaudible.

"Five *lire should* be your demand," she humbly ventured at last.

"Madame is quite right, but she forgets her three worships in the Cathedral and the many who partook of her bounty in the market!"

"Three worships," thought she with a perplexed air, "and bounties in the market!"

As if reading her mind, he explained by means of gestures that the contributions made in the church were charged to her, (probably with added interest by the time the account reached her;) also the coins given to the various mendicants in their walks.

Alas! A Quaker by parentage, educated to pay

no clergy in her own Protestant land, had here been playing into the hands of the foreign devotee! She nevertheless submitted with a grace, trusting that the next edition of Ollendorff will change its sentence of:

"Has he the hammer of the good blacksmith or the waistcoat of the handsome joiner," etc., into

"Has she the shrewdness of the saintly guide or the mask of the beggar in the market-place? She has neither the shrewdness of the saintly guide, neither the mask of the beggar; she has a meagre purse and a *"thorough lesson in Italian."*

FEEDING GHOSTS IN CHINA.

THE carpenter who has been making our new book-case says he wants to go to his home for a few days — some work is awaiting him there; the Chinese writer says *he* wishes to go — there is a message to be sent in the direction of his village, he can carry it, and, being at leisure, can spend a few days with his family; our house boy says *he*, also, must go — his "muddar" has been sick, is now "more better," and he must go and see her.

And so the carpenter and the writer have gone, and the boy is going; but it seems so strange, their all asking to go at the same time, that I suspect that at least part of them had some untold reason for it, and, when I remind myself that it is now the last of August, that it is the time of the full moon, and that last night our Chinese neighbors were going about out of doors carrying bowls of boiled rice, and that in front of the houses in the street near by were little fires with those thin, filmy ash-flakes that remain from burned paper scattered about them, I feel sure that I have guessed the reason, and that it is a wish to celebrate at their own homes the Festival of Burning Clothes, and the Friendless Ghost's Feast.

The Chinese think that persons after they are dead need the same things as when they are alive, and that if they are not supplied with them they can revenge themselves upon people in this world, bringing them ill-health or bad luck in business. This being the case, of course people try to keep the ghosts of their relations in as comfortable and quiet a state as they can.

If a father should die, his friends, while he remained unburied, would every day put a dish of rice and, perhaps, a basin of water, by his coffin, so that his ghost might eat and wash. Afterwards, they would at times carry food and drink to his grave, or place it before the wooden tablet, which, to honor

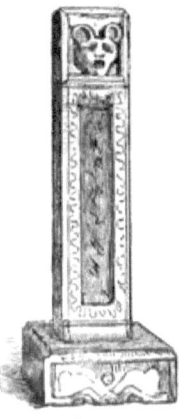

A Tablet.

him, would be set up in his house. To supply him with clothes and money, or anything else he might need, like a house, a boat or a chair, paper imitations of these things would be made and burned, after which it would be thought the ghost could make use of them. Fifteen days at this season of the year are considered the most lucky time for making these offerings. Large quantities of clothes and other paper articles are then sold, and there is a great burning of them all over the country.

Besides these well-to-do family ghosts, there is another class of whom people are dreadfully afraid. These are the spirits of very wicked men, and of childless persons who have left nobody behind them in this world to care for them. They are supposed to be wandering about in a most forlorn condition and to be able to do a great deal of mischief. To put them in good humor, and to induce them to keep out of the way of the living, a Feast is made for them every summer.

For several years past, this feast has been given in an open plot of ground just outside our yard and under our sitting-room windows, so that I have often seen it, though I am obliged to say I have never spied any ghosts coming to eat of it.

Every year the ceremonies are the same. Early in the day four tall poles are planted in the ground

THE GHOSTS' TABLE.

about a dozen feet apart, and so placed as to mark a square; about twenty feet from the ground a wooden floor is built between the poles. A few men who stand upon this platform direct everything. Usually, one or two of them seem to be priests; once, I recognized the leader as an expert juggler whose tricks

I had witnessed only a short time before. A part of the Feast has been made ready beforehand and is at once arranged on the platform. At two corners are placed ornamented cones, six or eight feet high, which, I suppose, it is expected will appear to the ghosts to be solid cakes, but which are, in reality, only bamboo frames, thinly plastered over with a mixture

A GHOST'S MEAL.

of flour and sugar; besides these are green oranges, other fresh fruits, and articles of different kinds. Soon, offerings of food begin to come in from the neighborhood, and are drawn up by ropes to the platform; these are, mostly, baskets of boiled rice, and have a bit of wood holding a red paper stuck in the middle of the rice. I suppose the giver's name is upon the paper, and after the Feast the baskets seem to be restored to the persons who brought them; the rice can then be taken away, and eaten at home.

At length, the platform is well laden with food, which remains exposed in the sun and wind for several hours, during which time a great noise is kept up with gongs and other musical instruments, partly, I suppose, like a dinner bell to call the ghosts, and partly to amuse the men and boys who gather in an interested crowd around the platform.

Late in the afternoon the head men begin to distribute the Feast. The baskets of food are carefully lowered; the cakes are broken up, and the pieces, with the oranges and other fruits, are flung hither and thither among the crowd, who scramble merrily after them, sometimes half a dozen rushing after the same fragment, and now and then a man trying to clamber up the poles to secure a portion before it falls. When the stage is cleared the crowd disperses, and the Ghosts' Feast is ended.

In this region the people are very poor, but in a large and rich community this festivity would be kept with splendor even, and with much cost.

Last year, a part of the wooden frame-work fell, and one man was injured. I think this may make the old ground seem unlucky to the Chinese, and lead them to seek a new place for this year's Feast.

Feeding Ghosts in China.

Let us hope that they will do so, for to have a set of the most wicked and unhappy ghosts asked to dinner under one's windows, is not, after all, so amusing as it is noisy and sadly foolish.

THE CHILDREN OF THE KOPPENBERG.

FROM Hanover to Hameln is a good twenty-five mile walk, with a mountain at the end: to go over which, however, shortens the journey by several miles.

In the case of Tom Osgood and Fred Taylor, who reached the foot of the mountain towards the close of what had been to them a long and weary day, the one — that is, Tom — concluded to go around the mountain, while Fred chose the shorter if rougher path over the top. Why the boys should have taken this long and tiresome tramp when a railroad runs the whole way in sight of the road which they travelled, or why they should not have walked to Hildesheim, or Mindem, or Nienburg, or any other of the equally unattractive places within the same distance from Hanover, I am sure I do not know. If they had, though — and for that matter if one of them had not chosen to climb the Koppenberg rather than go around it — this story would most likely have never been written.

For my own part I am very glad they did it; and Fred Taylor as long as he lives will never cease to be glad that he was the one to take the mountain path, though with the pleasure — as indeed is the case with nearly all our best pleasures — there will always come a little sudden thrill of pain.

Why the mountain was called the Koppenberg does not concern this story at all. It is quite enough to know that it was a pretty tough mountain to climb and that before Fred was a quarter of the way up he began to be sorry he had not taken the longer route with Tom. It was too late now however to turn back; and besides unless he made good time Tom would beat him in the race, which considering the greater distance Tom had to travel would be humiliating in the extreme. So putting a little extra steam in his legs, and whistling a tune his quick ear had picked up on the way, he trudged on, up the steep road, through the terraced vineyards, past an old ruin here and a herdsman's hut there, until finally the road lost itself in a path and went winding up into the

THE PIPER SOUNDED ONE SHARP NOTE.

woods which covered the mountain for more than half the distance from its top.

It was late in the afternoon; but in Hanover on the 26th of June the sun does not set until nearly half-past eight, so that Fred had no fear of being overtaken by the dark.

For some time Fred had not heard a sound but his own whistle. Indeed now that he was fairly in the solitude of the woods he did not expect to hear or meet any one, and he was accordingly startled when suddenly out of the deeper woods came a sound that seemed to be another whistle answering his own.

Fred stopped and listened.

Was it a whistle? or were they the notes of a flute?

At any rate it could be nothing dangerous. Highwaymen and banditti do not usually whistle or play musical instruments, and Fred felt that it would be perfectly safe to push on. As he drew nearer, the tones became louder and with them were mixed what were unmistakably the voices of children. Fred, with increasing curiosity, hastened his steps; and in another moment a sight that was as odd as it was pretty met his eyes.

Yes, they were children — as many as a hundred of them, Fred thought — funny little old-fashioned

German children; the girls with long flaxen braids and dresses that might have been their grandmothers', and the boys with garments so extraordinary that Fred, who thought he could never be astonished by what a German boy might have on, was fairly lost in surprise.

But more odd than all the rest was the musician himself — a tall, thin, smooth-faced man, with blue eyes and scanty hair and an astonishing cloak, half of yellow and half of red, that reached from his shoulders to his heels. He was playing, on what seemed to be a flageolet, a brisk enlivening tune, and was lightly beating time with his feet.

Fred looked on in amazement. "It must be a Sunday-school picnic," he said to himself at last, "only I never heard of such a thing in Germany, and what a queer-looking man for a superintendent."

If it were a Sunday-school picnic it was a very remarkable one. There were no grown-up people at all but the one man, and the children seemed to be having no end of a good time. There were two little girls, it is true, standing quietly and soberly not far from Fred, but all of the others were either dancing or playing some lively game.

Fred could not help wondering why the two were

left out; and going up to them he asked in his politest manner and best German: "Why aren't you dancing and why do you look so sad when everybody else is so happy?"

The little things looked up curiously. They were pretty, Fred thought, but not so pretty as another and older girl who came out of the crowd just then and overheard Fred's question.

"They've been sad all day," she answered in a pretty, motherly way; "their little brothers were left behind and they can't enjoy it because their brothers aren't enjoying it too."

"Mine was lame," said one of the little girls sadly.

"And mine was dumb," said the other.

"Oh come!" said Fred, "you'd better go in and have a dance. It will be getting dark before long and you'll have to go home and then you can tell your little brothers all about it."

The little children seemed puzzled and a grave look came on the elder girl's face.

"It is never dark," she said. "It is always light here."

It seemed indeed to be lighter than before. Where it had come from, Fred could not tell, but all the forest was lit up with a strange warm glow. There were beautiful flowers too growing at his feet and birds singing in the air that Fred had not noticed before.

"Won't you come and dance?" the girl went on.

Fred was very fond of dancing, and it was hard to refrain, especially since the music was now fairly exhilarating; but he was very tired and had still before him a tedious climb. Under the circumstances he would rather rest himself by talking to this pretty sweet-voiced German girl — if she would only stay.

"Well, to tell the truth," he said apologetically, "I've walked from Hanover to-day and I'm rather tired. But I'd like awfully to talk to you. Can't you stay away from them for a few minutes? You aren't a teacher, are you?"

"A teacher?" inquiringly.

"Yes. Isn't it a Sunday-school?"

"I don't think I understand."

Fred thought his German must be at fault.

"Well, I don't know," he said, "'*Sontags-schule*,' that's what they call it in New York. I've seen it on the German churches."

"New York? what is that?"

Fred gazed in greater astonishment.

"Now you don't mean to say you don't know where New York is?"

The girl shook her head in a dreamy, abstracted way.

"I have heard of Hameln," she said, "and Hanover, and Jerusalem where the Holy Sepulchre is. It was there the Count Rudolph went to war against the Turks. But he never came back. Do you know, eagerly, "whether the Christians have taken Jerusalem?"

"My gracious!" exclaimed Fred below his breath, "it must be a lunatic asylum!" Then aloud: "Why there hasn't been a war in Jerusalem for five hundred years — not since the crusades."

She passed her hand across her forehead in a bewildered way.

"I don't know, she said, "it seems as though I had forgotten. Perhaps it's because I don't talk. I'm the eldest, and all the others dance and play games, and the *Piper*, he plays all the time and so I don't have anybody to talk to at all."

Fred was now quite confirmed in his new idea; and yet the girl was so pretty and gentle that he could not bear to think of her being out of her mind.

"Why don't you go back," he asked kindly, "if

you're unhappy? Was it Hameln you came from?"

She shook her head.

"It was so long ago," she said, "I can't recollect."

"Well, it couldn't have been much over fourteen years. I'm only fifteen myself. Perhaps I'd ought to have introduced myself. I'm Fred Taylor, of New York and I'm studying German at Hanover. It's purer there, you know, than it is most anywhere else."

Fred was uncertain how much she understood. Her own language, he had noticed, was very simple, and when he used an unaccustomed word her forehead would contract as though she could not follow him. Her next words, though, showed that she had understood his introduction.

"I am Gretchen Haffelfinger," she said simply; "and you must not think I am not happy, because I am. The *Piper* is very kind to us."

"And do you live up here all the time?"

Her forehead contracted again.

"What is time?" she asked.

This was a problem that Fred wasn't prepared to solve and he discreetly changed the form of his question.

"Do you live near here?"

The girl's look turned toward a long glade in the forest, through which Fred fancied he could see a lofty castle with battlemented walls and windows that gleamed in the strange, rich glow.

"Is that the asylum?" he cried.

"I don't think I understand," wistfully.

What was there she did understand? Fred's heart warmed compassionately toward the simple-minded child, while a sudden thought came into his head. Once back in her own place — if Hameln were her own place — might not the familiar scenes bring back her scattered wits? Of the difficulties in the way he did not think.

"Say, Gretchen!" he whispered, eagerly, "wouldn't you like to go back with me to Hameln?"

A sudden light gleamed in the soft eyes and her breath came and went quickly as she moved a step nearer and looked beseechingly into his face. Fred will always insist that if they had started at that moment she would have gotten off. He reached forward, and for one instant her warm little hand lay in his. But before he could fairly grasp it, the *Piper* had sounded one clear, sharp note; the fingers that he so nearly held drew themselves away; the blue eyes which had been fixed on his, turned with a troubled look to the *Piper*; the slight form moved back, at first a single step, then slowly retreated from Fred's side, while the children, attracted by the same call, came running from all directions and formed in a double column behind their curiously dressed leader. In another moment the whole procession was in motion. Fred counted them mechanically as they filed by. Without Gretchen, who still delayed, or the *Piper*, there were just one hundred and twenty-nine.

What a weird intoxicating march it was! The children, for their part, laughed and sang; the *Piper* played as though he, too, were insane; and even Fred could scarcely resist the impulse to join in. If he did not get away he felt that he should be carried off by the music in spite of himself. But he would make at least one more effort to save his little friend.

"Gretchen!" he cried, holding out his hands.

She smiled, half sadly, and shook her head.

"Gretchen!" he cried once more, "come!"

There was no answer. The music had suddenly stopped, the *Piper* with the children had vanished; and, while Fred looked, the little maiden with the soft eyes and tender wistful smile faded out of his sight. The glow had gone, too, with the birds and the flowers; there was no longer any battlemented castle in the distance: it was the shade of the forest, and Fred was all alone.

Tom Osgood meanwhile had trudged his scarcely less weary way along the road around the foot of the mountain, and about seven o'clock had reached the city gate. Not that there was any gate — that had been gone for generations — but there was an old stone archway overgrown with ivy, in and out of which the birds fluttered and under which Tom had to walk to enter the city. Just before reaching it, he stopped for a moment and looked down into the river that flowed swiftly below the city walls. The sight struck a chord of recollection.

"What was it I used to read about this place?" he asked himself. "Seems to me it was in a piece I spoke once at school."

He waited a minute, but memory made no response. Then picking up his satchel he pushed on into the town.

To his surprise, when he had reached the hotel where they had agreed to meet, Fred was not there nor had anything been heard of him. The *Portier* assured Tom that the road was perfectly plain and nothing could have happened; but this did not altogether relieve him and it was with a good deal of anxiety, having ordered supper, that he sat down to wait. His suspense, however, did not last long. In fifteen minutes the door opened and Fred came in.

That something had happened, Tom guessed at once. There was a strange look of excitement on Fred's face, and his step was more active, Tom thought, than a boy's ought to be who had just walked over the Koppenberg.

"Feel my pulse, won't you, Tom?" he cried nervously, throwing down his satchel, "and see if I've got a fever. Did I seem out of my head when I left you? Did I talk wild, Tom? Did you ever hear of insanity in my family? Really and truly, Tom, I don't know whether I'm crazy or not."

Tom was gazing at his friend in speechless astonishment.

"What in the world's got into you?" he gasped.

"It didn't get into me. I got into it; and it was a lunatic asylum as near as I could make out. Only the keeper looked like a clown in a circus and the rest were all children. I tried to get one of them away, Tom"—Fred's voice broke a little—"but just then the whole thing vanished, just like people do in a dream, you know. I don't know where she went. I could see the spot where she stood, but she wasn't there — "

"Are you sure you weren't dreaming?" interrupted Tom.

"Dreaming!" indignantly. "Do I generally dream in daylight? Would I stop to dream when I was in such a hurry to get here ahead of you? and besides, Tom, I can whistle the march the man played. Just listen."

Fred was a good whistler and never had to hear a tune more than once to remember it perfectly. Now his excitement lent strength and clearness to his notes so that any one might have taken them for those of the *Piper* himself. So loud and clear were they indeed that the *Portier* was drawn by them from his desk, the *Ober-kellner* from the dining-room, the Director from the office, and most of the guests from the reading and smoking rooms. In fact, before Fred was through he had quite an audience, most of whom, he noticed, had a puzzled, inquiring look on their faces as though something about the whistle or the tune were out of the way. What the look meant he did not have to wait long to find out.

"You whistle very well, sir," the Director remarked, almost before Fred was fairly through; "but perhaps you are not aware that that tune is forbidden in Hameln."

Fred was surprised, and a little frightened.

"Why," he stammered, "I only learned it to-day."

"Not from any one in Hameln?"

"No, I don't suppose it was. He was on the other side of the mountain."

The Director shook his head sagaciously.

"It is not allowed in Hameln," he repeated; "I wouldn't whistle it again if I were you."

"But why not?" demanded Fred. "Why can't a man whistle what he likes?"

"For the same reason," gravely, "that it is forbidden to play music of any kind in the *Bungenstrasse.*"

Fred stared.

"What is the *Bungenstrasse?*" he asked; "and why may not one play in it?"

"Do not the young *herren* know the story?"

The young *herren* did not know the story, or if they did had forgotten it.

"Is there a story?" cried Tom. "Tell it to us, won't you, Herr Director?"

The Director bowed gravely.

"Probably the young *herren* will recall it, for one

of their English poets has written about it. It happened nearly six hundred years ago that the town of Hameln was overrun with rats—"

That was enough. Tom had found his clue.

"Of course I've read it!" he cried. "That was what I've been trying to remember all day:

>"'Hamelin town's in Brunswick,
>   By famous Hanover city;
>The River Weser, deep and wide,
>Washes its wall on the southern side'—

Don't you recollect, Fred? They couldn't get rid of them, and one day an old fellow came into town and offered to pipe them out for a thousand dollars or whatever it was, and they took him up. But when he had done it, and the rats were all drowned in the river, they wouldn't stick to the bargain, and so he struck up his pipe again, and this time all the children followed him—why, what's the matter, Fred?"

"The young gentleman is ill," exclaimed the *Portier*, and would have rushed off for a doctor, had not Fred interfered.

"No! no!" impatiently, "I'm not sick, Tom; but don't you see? Is it so?" turning to the Director, "Is that the story?"

The Children of the Koppenberg.

The Director nodded. He was flattered by their interest, and besides nothing that an American did ever surprised him.

"Evidently the young gentleman has read it," he said. "All the children in town followed him as far as the mountain side, and then, when their fathers and mothers thought they could go no further, the mountain opened and they were all swallowed up — all, that is, but one little boy who was dumb, and another who was lame. This was the street they went down. On the *Rattenfangerhauser* opposite is a tablet commemorating the event; and ever since that time there has been no music played in the *Bungenstrasse*. Even if a bridal procession goes through the street the music must not play. And the tune which you were whistling was the tune the Piper played. It was scored at the time by the *Kapellmeister*, and every one in Hameln knows it, just as one knows the *Wacht am Rhein;* but no one may play it, or whistle it, or sing it on the streets. Of course, if the young gentleman had known it was forbidden he would not have whistled it."

"Of course not," said Fred, abstractedly. "Where is the house with the inscription on it? Can we see it?"

"Certainly," said the Director. "It is not yet too dark. The house is yonder on the corner of the *Osterstrasse*."

By this time Tom was burning with curiosity, and longing for a chance to speak with Fred alone.

"Come along," he cried, "let's go over to the old place and look at it."

Fred was not unwilling, and tired and hungry though they were, both boys rushed out of the hall across the Platz. The hotel people interchanged smiles and shrugs, the *Ober-kellner* went back to the dining-room, the *Portier* to his desk, the Director to his office and the guests to their rooms. "Americans!" one said to the other, quite as though that dismissed the subject.

In the few minutes which it took to cross the square, Fred gave his friend all the particulars of the story which in his excitement he had not before supplied, and for lack of which Tom had not been able until now to obtain a clear idea of what had happened. "Then your idea is," he said soberly, when Fred had finished, "that those were the children who were lost?"

Fred nodded gravely. "I suppose they must have been," he said.

"And that the man was the Pied Piper of Hameln?"

Fred nodded as before. By this time they were in front of the house and had discovered the inscription, which was written in queer old characters, once gilded, but now so weather beaten as to be scarcely legible.

"What in the world does it

THE RAT-CATCHER'S HOUSE.

say?" asked Tom.

Fred scanned it as closely as he could in the fading light.

The Children of the Koppenberg.

"It's hard to tell," he said. Part of it is Latin and part German; but it's badly spelled, and there is some of it that must be Dutch. As near as I can make out it reads like this:

"*Anno* 1284 *am dage Johannis et Pauli war der* 26 *Junii dorch einen Piper mit allerlei farve bekledet gewesen* 130 *Kinder verledet binnen Hameln gebon to Calvarie, bi den Koppen verloren!*"

"What gibberish!" Tom exclaimed. "Do you suppose you can translate it?"

Fred looked uncertain; but began word by word, as one construes a Latin lesson in school.

"*Anno* 1284, in the year 1284, *am dage Johannis et Pauli*, on the day of St. John and St. Paul, *war der* 26 *Junii*, which was the 26th of June — this very day, Tom — a piper with *allerlei farve bekledet* — that must be parti-colored clothes — led 130 children born in Hameln by the Koppenberg to Calvary. That means to their death I suppose."

Tom nodded, and for a minute the boys looked at one another without speaking.

"Well, what are you going to do about it?" asked Tom at length.

With another look at the tablet Fred turned towards the hotel.

The Children of the Koppenberg.

"There's nothing to be done about it," he said. "I don't think I had better tell anybody here."

Tom deliberated a minute.

"No, I don't think you had," he said. "It happened five hundred and ninety-five years ago: there aren't any of their relatives alive, and nobody would believe you anyhow. Besides, they seemed to be having a good time, didn't they?"

Fred's thoughtful gaze was turned down the street toward the mountain, where so many years ago the little feet had pattered to their grave.

But *was* it to their grave?

He wondered if instead of dying they had not lived all that time, and whether any one else had ever seen them besides himself. He was so absorbed indeed that he did not hear Tom's question until it was repeated.

"Oh, did you speak?" he asked. "Yes, I suppose they were. She said so."

"Well, I'm glad of that. I always felt sorry for the poor little beggars and wondered if they got out of the other side of the hill. It's a great relief, Fred, to think of their having a good time. The Piper couldn't have been a bad sort of fellow. As it turned out, Fred, you might say as the little lame boy — it must have been his sister, by the way, you spoke to—did in the poem:

> 'The music stopped and I stood still,
> And found myself outside the hill,
> Left alone against my will,
> To go now limping as before,
> And never hear of that country more.'"

Fred drew a long breath of relief as he brought his thoughts back from the mountain.

"Well," he said, "I'm glad I know who they were. I couldn't bear to think of their being lunatics. And if Gretchen and the two little girls had been as happy as all the rest, I should have thought —"

"What would you have thought?"

Fred hesitated an instant.

"That I was getting a little glimpse into heaven. But then, it couldn't be that, you know."

Tom shook his head wisely.

"Oh, no," he said; "of course it couldn't be that."

A DAY AT THE BUTTS.

IT was the fourth day of August, more than a hundred years ago, and the whole road between London and the little village of Harrow was thronged with people. It was hot and dusty enough that summer morning, but nobody seemed to mind in the eager scramble for the best seats; and it was not long before the little green knoll, just at the west of the London road, seemed fairly alive with spectators.

It was a lovely spot — this well-known Butts of Harrow — with its crown of tall forest trees waving like so many banners, and its tiers of grassy seats terracing the slope. From time immemorial it had been the scene of annual contests in archery, and there was not a boy in Harrow School who did not look forward all the year to this fourth day of August.

A Day at the Butts.

When John Lyon founded the school it was made a condition of entrance, that every pupil should be furnished with the proper implements of archery; and among the school ordinances drawn up in the year 1592 there was one to the effect that every child should, at all times, be allowed bow-shafts, bow-strings, and a bracer.

No wonder the men of those days were tall, and straight, and strong!

But hark! The church clock down in the village is striking the appointed hour. A little figure, clad in red satin from head to foot, darts out from the thicket of trees below, and now a procession of twelve boys, some in white, some in red, and some in green satin, take their places in the open ring that has been left for the competitors. All the little archers have sashes and caps of bright-colored silk, and, looking down from the green knoll, the whole scene is a kaleidoscope of color.

A silver arrow — the victor's prize — glitters temptingly in the sunlight; and a tall lad, who stands among the waiting twelve, bends eagerly forward to examine it.

"Just look at Percival!" whispers one little archer to his neighbor. "He's bound to get that arrow, isn't he?"

"Pooh! who cares for the arrow?" responds the other, disdainfully. "It's nothing but a plaything, anyway! What I think about is winning the game, not the arrow!"

"Yes; but you see it's different with Percival!" said the first speaker. "His three older brothers, three years in succession, won the arrows while they were here at the Harrow School, and the father says that Percival must win the fourth for the one empty corner in the drawing-room, or he shall be ashamed to call him his son!"

Just here the boys were interrupted in their talk, for the target was ready, and, at a signal, the contest began. At first, one shot after another fell quite outside the third circle that surrounded the bull's-eye, then came a shaft that glanced just to one side of the inner circle; but at last, after many fruitless attempts, the bull's-eye was fairly pierced, and the feat was greeted with a gay concert from the French horns.

Now, it so happened — at least this is one of the traditions of Harrow — that the name of this last boy was "Love," and when his arrow touched the bulls-eye a number of his school-fellows shouted high above the horns:

"*Omnia vincit Amor!*"

"Not so!" said another boy who stood close by. "*Nos non cedamus Amori!*" And, carefully adjusting his shaft, he shot it into the bull's-eye a whole inch nearer the centre than his rival.

But each boy among the twelve competitors must have his own trial shot twelve times repeated, before the final award can be given. Meanwhile a careful tally is kept, and not until the one hundred and forty-fourth arrow springs from its bow is the victor's name announced:

"Thomas Reginald Percival."

That first victory seems to have given a magic impulse to his bow, for all twelve of his arrows have pierced the charmed inner circle of the target; and now, at the head of an excited procession of boys, he is borne triumphantly from the Butts to the village. One little fellow in white satin runs far ahead, waving the silver arrow with many flourishes; and, when the school-buildings of Harrow are reached, a grand reception is given to all the neighboring country-folk.

Young Percival, with bright eyes and flushed cheeks, is the hero of the evening. There are games and dancing, and all sorts of merry-making until the "wee sma" hours, but the victorious boy can think of nothing save the coveted arrow he has won. That empty corner no longer troubles his excited brain.

He has ably vindicated his right to the old family name, and henceforward, the father can point with pride to four trophies, won by his four sons at the famous Butts of Harrow.

That was in 1766. In 1771 the annual shootings at Harrow were abolished; for Dr. Heath, who was then head-master of the school, thought they interfered with the boys' studies. The silver arrow prepared for the following year, 1772, was never used, but is still preserved at Harrow as a relic of the past. In the school-library may be seen one of the archer's elaborate suits, which is nearly a hundred years old; and the fourth of August, though no longer an exciting day at the Butts, is still kept as a holiday at Harrow School, and commemorated with appropriate speeches.

TINY FEET OF CHINESE LADIES.

JUST imagine the foot of a full grown lady but five inches in length! Yet even this is large, and in highly aristocratic families four inches is the standard.

This queer custom of compressing the feet of Chinese girls is of very ancient date, and in our day is almost universal — only nuns, slaves, boat-women, and others who are obliged to perform out-door drudgery, being exempt. As to the origin of the custom, the Chinese themselves are not agreed. Many suppose that it is a fashion intended to draw a line between the higher and lower classes. Others say that its object was to keep *ladies* within doors, where they would not be subjected, like common market or boat-women, to the gaze of the other sex; and some boldly declare that to cripple them was known to be the only way by which women could be kept at home, and rendered of use working for their husbands or fathers, instead of spending their time in gadding and gossip. Some of the most reliable native historians state that the custom began during the reign of Take, somewhere about the year 1123, with a whim of the last Empress of the Shang dynasty.

The time for putting on the first bandages varies in different families. In some, the process is commenced when the baby is only a few weeks old, others defer the ceremony for a year or two; but all begin before the little one has reached the age of four years.

No iron or wooden shoe is used, as some travelers have stated; but a strip of cotton cloth, some three inches wide, and about six feet long, is wound around the toes, over the instep, and then behind the heel, after which it is brought back again over the foot and drawn so tightly around the toes as to press them into a point—all except the first and second having been previously doubled under the sole.

These bandages are never removed, except for purposes of cleanliness, perhaps once a month; and they are replaced as quickly as possible, each time being drawn tighter, until the instep bends into a bow and the ball of the foot is forced against the heel.

The stockings are made of white cotton or silk.

The dainty little shoes are of silk, richly embroidered and often beautifully adorned with tiny pearls or rubies. The soles are of white satin, quilted, and stiffened with a lining of pasteboard. The heels are very high and pointed, and the white satin that entirely covers them, as well as the upturned toes, presents a pretty contrast to the blue or crimson silk uppers.

White satin seems to us an odd material for shoe soles; but they are intended only for carpeted floors.

When one of these tiny satin-soled slippers is cast off as "worn out," it has probably never for a single time come in contact with *terra firma*; and probably the wearer, when robed in the white slippers for her last sleep, has not from her infancy had one gleeful romp out-doors.

This compression produces, during all the years of childhood, the most excruciating pain, followed at length by a sort of numbness. I never saw one of these compressed feet entirely without covering, but I saw enough when the outer bandages had been removed to excite both pity and disgust; and a lady who had seen the bare foot of one of their greatest belles told me that she had never even conceived of a spectacle so shockingly revolting as this tiny foot when divested of all that could hide its deformity. Although the young lady was full grown, the sole of

Tiny Feet of Chinese Ladies.

her foot was but three and three-quarters inches in length. The great toe formed a point that was bent upwards and backwards, while the heel, of natural size, seemed by contrast disproportionately large.

Chinese ladies of rank are seldom seen abroad unless in closely curtained Sedan-chairs; but we used occasionally to meet those of the middle class making short excursions in the immediate vicinity of their homes. Their attempts at walking were pitiable in the extreme, as they hobbled along, leaning on an umbrella, or the shoulder of a servant, for support, or with hands outstretched against the houses as they passed, endeavoring to keep their balance.

SHETLAND PONIES.

F AR north from Scotland, and but seldom visited by southern travelers are the Shetland Islands. From these rock-bound, treeless islands come the Shetland ponies that we so often see at the circus, or pulling little phaetons patiently along. A Shetland pony is almost a child's first desire, unless, perhaps, it may be to own a monkey. To have a pony to ride, or to drive, and especially a *real* Shetland, long-haired, short-legged pony is a dream of perfect happiness, indeed.

But have the readers of this little sketch ever thought about the home of these ponies? If you never have, then take a map of the British Isles, and in the far North you will see the small group of islands called the Shetlands, and from there the first ponies came; and to-day they are raised there in great numbers.

Shetland is a very different country than many see. There are no green fields and trees, and the children living there hardly believe it when you tell them that in England or Scotland there are green lanes, and that birds build nests among green leaves. All the birds they see, hover about the great, rocky cliffs, and build nests in the crevices of rocks, perhaps a thousand feet above the sea. All their fields are covered with black peat or brown heather; and instead of houses of wood to live in, they only have huts made of stone with a roof of straw, mud and refuse wood. In some of the houses there are no windows, only one room, and a low door. Then there is no chimney to let the smoke out, but only a small hole in the roof. Of course these huts are for the very poor people living out among the hills of Shetland, and away from the coast. But near the sea, on the shores of some secluded bay, are quite good towns, such as Lerwick and Scolloway. These towns have little stone houses with very pointed roofs and deep-set windows, that almost seem to rest in the water itself, they are built so near it. Then the streets are very narrow, and have been paved with great stones. You can almost touch either side of the street it is so narrow.

Now the people of the Shetland Islands are very quiet, orderly and industrious. They live by many means. Some of them have shops in the towns, where they sell groceries, and dress-goods and cured meats. Others live by catching fish to send south. Some let themselves down by ropes over the edge of a great high cliff, and gather the eggs of birds. Then the women knit shawls and hoods and veils and socks, and so gain a few pennies to buy food with. But there is yet another class of people who have to make a living, and this class raise ponies and sheep, to send to England and even to America. And before we speak or describe carefully the making of shawls and gathering of eggs, we will imagine ourselves in the town of Lerwick and all ready for a start to Noss Island, where a man lives who has a large herd of real Shetland ponies.

I remember the morning perfectly. The bay was all dotted with the white sails of the fishing boats. The town was all awake carrying dried fish to the boats at anchor, and on the corners of the streets were gathered women and young girls selling potatoes they had just brought in from the distant field. We took a row boat, and rowed across Bressay Sound to Bressay Island, and then walking across it, and after looking back at the town and out at sea, we came to a small strait, and had to hire another boat to take us across the water to Noss Island. This island is not very large, but has more green grass than any other of the Shetland group. One end of it almost buries itself in the sea, and then it gradually rises higher and higher, until the opposite end rises a thousand feet right up from the sea. There is only

SHETLAND PONIES.

one house on the island, and in that lives the keeper of the ponies and his two children. I wish you could have seen these children when they saw us coming in the boat. They hardly ever leave the island themselves, and so when any strangers come to see their ponies, how happy it makes them! They were very pretty and bright children, too. They had light hair and bright blue eyes, and cheeks as red as roses. Running down with them, was their pet dog, who seemed just as glad as any of the rest to see strangers. The house the man lived in was very lonely-looking to us. It was built of stone, and then painted white, and stood on a little knoll overlooking the blue waters of the cold North Sea.

After a short rest we walked out to explore the island and see the ponies. Here was their home and we should see them here in their real life. As we walked along, we came to a part of the island where it was rather sandy, and there found such a nest of rabbits. We almost stumbled into their holes, there were so many of them when we came upon them. There must have been fully a hundred nibbling the short grass, or standing up to see who was coming to disturb them. The keeper said they were a great nuisance to the island, they undermined it so.

Shetland Ponies.

But a sight that interested us more than that of the rabbits was the great herd of ponies we saw before us.

There must have been fully two hundred of the shaggy-maned little fellows. Some were eating, some biting one another, some running as though having a race, and others stood still looking at us. When we came nearer the whole herd pricked up their ears, gave little snorts of anger, and galloped away as fast as their short legs could carry them.

The keeper told us that when one wishes a pony, to ride or sell, he must take the one he keeps near his house, mount him, and then riding out to the herd, lassoo one at a time until you obtain all you wish. In winter the ponies of Noss Island have rather a hard time of it. Though there is not much snow on the island, still the winds often blow very fiercely, and poor pony has no warm barn to go to. Sometimes the keeper builds a wall about a square piece of ground, and pony can go into the enclosure and so be somewhat sheltered. But usually he must face the wind and storm, no matter what the weather.

Among the ponies we saw on our visit, were some little wee fellows, hardly larger than Newfoundland dogs. When we saw them scampering about so free from care, we couldn't help wondering how long it would be before they would be carrying some little lady up and down Rotten Row, or about New York Central Park. The case is not unlikely, for a great many of them each year are sent away from their island home to England.

But a pony in the Shetland Islands, even, has often hard work to perform. If a poor person is possessed of a pony, then, indeed, he feels rich. Now on certain days in the week, there are market days at Lerwick. From all about come the people bringing things to sell. Some walk to the town, some sail, and others come riding on their ponies. Just inside of Lerwick is a narrow path leading over the hills. I have often seen, coming along this narrow way, a long line of ponies and women. And such a curious appearance they present! The ponies seem only legs. They have no bridle, only a cord about the neck, and each follows the one in front. You can't make them go at the side of one another. On either side of each one are two immense saddle-bags filled with peat, or potatoes; on his back are piled other goods, and even his neck has a cloth or other saddle-bags strapped, so that seen from a short distance it seems just as though the bags had legs, and poor pony seems buried out of sight. Sometimes, too, if there is room to keep seated, his mistress, with shoeless feet, and short dress and white cap, seats herself in great state, and away goes pony, bags and woman, off to Lerwick. Sometimes, when on these pilgrimages, pony will watch his chance, and if his mistress should be absent, will dart away down the steep hill-side, to nibble a bite of something good he has seen; and then when the mistess sees him such a pounding as pony gets as she leads him back to his proper place! But he only looks meek and will no doubt do the same thing again when he gets the chance.

Shetland ponies are very sure-footed. They will walk along the very edge of a high cliff, and before putting a foot down will carefully feel if the ground is firm or not. Some of them are driven by their riders down steep passes where one misstep would send both rider and pony down to the depths below. Ponies of Shetland, too, are not always very well behaved. Near our cottage was an old lady's garden, filled with cabbages. One day her pony walked into it, and enjoyed himself feasting on the forbidden fruit. We never asked him, but should imagine the beating he received when discovered would help him to digest his stolen dinner. Then a Shetland pony on his native heath is extremely wilful. If they dislike a rider they will spare no pains to unseat him. I rode one once who expended a great deal of unnecessary strength in this manner. He would sit down suddenly and rise up more so. He would bite, shake himself and roll over, if allowed. As he was almost small enough to be carried by his rider, these antics were more amusing than dangerous.

And so the ponies of the Shetland Islands live and wait for masters in the South. In the cold winter of fog and rain, when there is almost no day, or in the summer time, when the sun does not set, they run wild about the Noss, take burdens to Lerwick, or carry the stranger over the bogs and dreary hills.

MR. SWEET POTATOES.

OUR milkman has a very odd name, — translated into English it is "Sweet Potatoes." His Chinese neighbors call him "Old Father Sweet Potatoes."

Some persons think him a good man; others say that he is a very bad one. Just how that is I do not know — his business brings him great temptation.

He is accused of putting water into the milk. He himself says, that he only does it when he has not enough milk to supply all his customers; then he does not know what else he *can* do. When we engaged him to bring milk to us we took him into our yard and showed him that we had a well of our own.

The Chinese in their own country do not make any use of milk or butter. They have a perfect horror of cheese, and in this part of China, perhaps, not more than one man in a hundred will taste of beef. Only a few cows and bullocks are kept, and these are needed to plough the fields and turn the rude machinery of the sugar mills.

I suppose "Father Sweet Potatoes" had never thought of such a thing as owning a cow, until foreign ships began to come to his part of the country. Of course the ships brought foreign men and women, and these all wanted beef to eat — sometimes the Chinese, wishing to speak contemptuously of them, would call them "beef-eating foreigners," — and they also wanted milk for their cooking and for their children.

So Mr. Sweet Potatoes bought some cows, hoping to make some money in the milk business. They all had long ropes laced about their horns or threaded through their noses, and he got some little children to hold the ropes and guide the cows in search of food; for there are no grass fields in this part of the country, and all the pastures the cows have are the little green places on the rocky hills and the grassy patches along the brooks; and the children sit by and watch them while they graze, for there are no fences, and, left to themselves, the cows might stray into the rice fields or wander away into places where they would be stolen.

Mr. Sweet Potatoes.

Strange to say, we have our best milk when the winter has almost killed the grass, or when the weather is too stormy for the cows to go out; for then they are fed with the tops of pea-nut plants,

THE NATIVE HUMPBACK COW.

either green, or dried like hay, and up for sale in great bundles. This is delicious food for the cows, and when they have it then we have good milk indeed, with a thick, white cream upon it.

Sometimes they have cut grass to eat, which has

been brought from steep places on the hills to which the cows cannot go. Very poor boys go out with baskets and knives to gather this grass, and are paid only three or four cents for the work of a day.

Mr. Sweet Potatoes has two kinds of cows. Some of them are the native humpback cows, of very small size, very gentle; sometimes red and sometimes brown, with hair that is smooth and glossy quite down to the tiny little hoofs, which look far smaller and cleaner than do the feet of cows in colder climates where they walk out in snow and stand in frosty barns.

These cows have very small horns, sometimes three or four inches long, but often mere little white buds coming out from their dark foreheads. Back of their shoulders they have a small hump, three or four inches high. And, almost always, Sweet Potatoes' cows have with them a pretty, little, sprightly calf; for the Chinese believe, or pretend to believe, that if the calf were taken away the cow would die, and that it is necessary before milking her to first let the calf have a few mouthfuls of milk, — poor little calf!

The other cows are very different from these; they are water buffaloes, — buffaloes not at all like the shaggy bison, but great, awkward creatures, that in summer like to wade into pools, and, safe from flies and mosquitos, to stand with only their horns and upturned faces in sight above the top of the water; or, when there are no pools, to wander into bogs and half bury themselves in the mud. They are as large as a big ox, with very round bodies mounted on very slim legs that have very large knee and ankle joints. They are of the color of a mouse, or a gray pig, and coarse hairs grow thinly over their skin, while, in contrast to the humpback cows, they have two immense, crescent-shaped horns setting up from their heads, and measuring often a yard from side to side.

Old Father Sweet Potatoes sells ten pint-bottles full for a silver dollar, — that is ten cents a pint, — and in summer he brings us a half-pint in the morning and another half-pint in the afternoon; for the weather is so hot that the milk of the morning will not remain sweet until evening, although the moment it is brought to the house it is boiled and then put in the coolest place we have, which is not a cellar, for cellars cannot be kept sweet and airy in countries where there is so much moisture and many insects.

When, in our walks, we meet these cows they often exhibit fear, especially of foreign ladies and horses, sights with which they are not familiar. The little humpback cows prance skittishly out of the paths; but the great buffaloes stand quite still and stare at

Mr. Sweet Potatoes.

us, then throw up their noses and sniff the air in an offended manner that in turn makes us afraid of them.

At night they are all brought home from their wanderings, and the ropes by which they are led are tied

THE WATER-BUFFALO.

to stakes driven into the ground; in winter under a shed, but in summer in the open air. It makes one's neck ache to see them; for the rope is frequently tied so short that they cannot hold their heads erect nor move them very freely, but they do not appear to suffer.

Mr. Sweet Potatoes.

Next to his business the milkman values his daughter, who, when I first saw her, was a plump, rosy-cheeked child and tended her father's cows. If you ever saw a doll with a plaster head that had been broken and then had been mended by having a strip of black silk glued over the crack, you will know how Mr. Sweet Potatoes' daughter looked.

She wore a piece of black crape bound tightly about her head so that no one could see her hair. Some persons said that, owing to illness, she had no hair. If so it must have grown afterwards; for, when she was older and had left tending the cows, she had it put up on her head with pins, in a strange fashion that showed she was going to be married.

Sweet Potatoes had no son and he wished his son-in-law to come and live with him as if he belonged to him. Among the Chinese this is not considered so honorable or so genteel, as to have the daughter leave her home and go and live with her husband's family. It seemed strange that the son-in-law should consent; for though he was very poor he was also very proud, and was very particular to have respect shown to him and in regard to the kinds of work that he was willing to do. I should never have guessed his foolish reason for being so proud, but some one told me that it was because his father, now dead, had once held a small office in the Custom House!

SHETLAND WOMEN.

NOT far outside the town of Lerwick, on the Shetland Islands there is a great, black, muddy tract of land called a peat-bog. All about is utter desolation. There are no huts even to be seen. The town is concealed by a rounded hill; and when, through some opening between the bare upheavals, one catches a sight of the North Sea, it, too, seems deserted by mankind.

The peat, or mixture of roots and peculiar black soil, is dug here in large quantities; and all about the place are great piles of it, dried and ready to be burned in the fire-places of the Lerwick people. Peat takes the place of wood; and in every poor man's hut in Shetland will it be found burning brightly, and giving out a thin blue smoke.

To prepare peat for market, a great deal of labor is performed. First come the diggers — men, women and children. Entering upon the deep, miry bogs they cut the soil up into cakes about a foot long and a few inches thick; and these they place in high piles to dry. After a few weeks they come again, and carry the cured fuel away to the town.

It is while carrying these loads that the Shetlanders present a peculiar spectacle. The men are often very old, infirm and poorly clothed; and the women are dressed in short-skirted, home-spun gowns, below which may be seen very red and very broad feet. On their heads they usually have white caps, nicely ironed, with a fluted ruffle around the edge. Passing across the breast and over either shoulder are two strong straps, and these support an immense basket hanging against the back.

Thus equipped, the brave, stout women, their baskets piled with peat, tramp off to Lerwick, two miles away, to sell their loads for a few pennies each. They make many trips a day, always smiling, chatting and apparently contented. Often a long line may be seen carefully stepping along over the rough roads, stopping now and then to rest.

The homes of these poor peat women are, many of them, simply hovels. When they wish to build a

COAST OF SHETLAND

Shetland Women.

home, they go out into some fields, usually far away from other huts, and there they dig a trench about a

SHETLAND WOMEN.

square piece of ground. Upon this they build walls to a height of about eight feet, and fill the crevices with mud and bog. For a roof they gather refuse sea-wood, and, with this for a support, lay on layer after layer of straw, mud and stones.

But what homes they seem to us! There is no fire-place, only a hole in the ground, with a hole in the roof for the smoke to escape through! No windows, the door serving for both light and entrance! No beds, only heaps of straw! Sometimes in one small room, often the only one the house contains, will be seen man, wife, children, dog and hens, equal occupants, sharing the same rude comforts. Outside the house, if the owner be moderately well off, may be seen a herd of sheep or ponies, and a patch of garden surrounded by a wall.

But there is something a peat woman of Shetland is continually doing that we have not yet noticed. All have no doubt heard of Shetland hosiery; of the fine, warm shawls and hoods, and delicate veils that come from these far northern islands. Now, all the while the poor, bare-legged woman is carrying her heavy burden of peat, her hands are never idle. She is knitting, knitting away as fast as her nimble fingers will allow. In her pocket is the ball of yarn, and as her needles fly back and forth, she weaves fabrics of such fineness that the Royal ladies of England wear them; and no traveller visits the island without loading his trunk with shawls, mittens, stockings, and other feminine fancies.

Not to know how to knit in Shetland is like not knowing how to read at home. A little girl is taught the art before she can read; and, as a result, at every cottage will be found the spinning-wheel and the needles, while the feminine hands are never idle. It is one great means of support; and on Regent Street in London will be seen windows full of soft, white goods marked "Shetland Hosiery."

Who first instructed these far northern people in this delicate art is not surely known. On Fair Isle, one of the Shetland group, the art is first said to have been discovered, very many years ago. On that lonely isle even now, every woman, girl and child knits while working at any of her various duties.

The yarn with which the Shetland goods are made is spun from the wool of the sheep we see roaming about the fields. In almost every cottage may be seen the veritable old-fashioned wheel; and the busy girl at the treadle sends the great wheel flying, and spins out the long skeins, which serve to make baby pretty hood or grandma a warm shawl.

MARDI GRAS IN NICE.

HAVE you ever happened in Nice at Carnival?

On a bright June morning, which my calendar called February twelfth, Rull and I tripped lightly down through the old olive orchards to the station, and billeted ourselves for Nice.

Long before we reached Nice Rull's hands tingled; for there lay a beautiful line of snow, miles away, on the *north* side of the Alps, and the poor fellow hadn't been as near a snow-ball as that for the winter. But I had only to say "*confetti!*" and his eyes danced at the vision of the parti-colored hail-storm to come.

Mardi Gras In Nice.

Now hasten with us at once to the *Promenade du Cours*, up and down which the procession is to pass.

First, however, I shall buy for you each a little blue gauze mask; for you cannot even peep at Carnival unmasked. And if any of you can wear linen dusters with hoods attached, all the better. Don't

"PROMENADE DU COURS," IN CARNIVAL TIME.

leave a square inch of skin unprotected, I warn you.

Besides the little masks, you may buy, each of you, a whole bushel of these "sugar-plums," and have them sent to our balcony. Also for each a little tin scoop fastened on a flexible handle, which you are to fill with *confetti* but on no account to pull — at least, not yet.

The crowds are gathering. Pretty peasant girls in their holiday attire of bright petticoats, laced bodices, and white frilled caps; stray dominoes; richly dressed ladies with mask in hand; carriages so decorated with flowers as to be artistically hidden — even the wheels covered with batiste — blue, pink, purple, green or buff. Even the sidewalk, as we

" PROMENADE DU COURS " IN CARNIVAL TIME.

pass, is fringed with chairs at a franc each.

The "*Cours*" is gay with suspended banners, bright with festooned balconies and merry faces. Sidewalks and street are filled with people; but the horses have the right of way, and the people are fined if they are run over.

Let us hasten to our balcony, for here passes a

band of musicians, in scarlet and gold, to open the procession.

Just in time we take our seats, and lo! before us rolls a huge car.

It is "the theatre"—an open car of puppets—but the puppets are *men;* all attached to cords held in the hand of the giant, who sits in imposing state

"PROMENADE DU COURS," IN CARNIVAL TIME.

above them on the top of the car which is on a level with the third story balconies.

The giant lifts his hand and the puppets whirl and jump. But alas! his head is too high. His hat is swept off by the hanging festoons, and the giant must ride bare-headed, in danger of sunstroke.

Next behind the car moves in military order a

regiment of mounted grasshoppers. Their sleek, shining bodies of green satin, their gauzy wings and antennæ, snub noses and big eyes, are all absolutely perfect to the eye ; but — they are of the size of men.

You lower your mask to see more clearly, you are lost in wonder at the perfect illusion, your mouth is wide open with "Ohs!" and "Ahs!" when *pop!*

"PROMENADE DU COURS" IN CARNIVAL TIME.

pop! slings a shower of *confetti*, and the little hailstones seem to cut off your ears and rush sifting down your neck.

For, while you were watching the grasshoppers, a low open carriage, concealed under a pink and white cover, has stopped under our windows. Four merry masqueraders, cloaked and hooded in hue to match, have a bushel of *confetti* between them, and are piled with nosegays. We slink behind our masks, we pull the handles of our *confetti* scoops — then the battle begins and waxes fierce.

But they are crowded on; for behind them, in irresistible stateliness, moves on the Sun and Moon. Then come the Seasons: Winter represented by a

"PROMENADE DU COURS," IN CARNIVAL TIME.

band of Russians, fur-covered from top to toe, dragging a Siberian sledge. Summer is recognized by a car-load of choicest flowers, whose fragrance reaches us as they pass.

Here rolls a huge wine cask which fills half the wide street; there moves a pine cone, six feet high, to the eye perfectly like the cones, six inches in length, which we use daily to light our olive-wood fire.

Then a procession of giant tulips — stalk, calyx, petals, all complete. They also silently move on.

Next a huge pot, with a cat climbing its side, her paw just thrust beneath the lid. Ha! it suddenly flies off. Does the cat enter? We cannot see through the crowd. A colossal stump follows, trail-

"PROMENADE DU COURS," IN CARNIVAL TIME.

ing with mosses and vines. Upon it a bird's nest filled with young, their mouths wide open for food; wonderful, because the artistic skill is so perfect that, although so immense, they seem living and not unnatural.

Then a car of Arctic bears champing to and fro in the heat, poor things, as well they may; for this is a cloudless sky and an Italian sun. Look carefully at them and tell me, are they not true bears?

But ah! *sling! sling!* two handfuls of *confetti* sting your eyes back into place again, and dash the bears out of sight. Isn't it delightfully unbearable? You shout at the folly of having forgotten *confetti*, and then resolve to watch your chance at the next poor

" PROMENADE DU COURS " IN CARNIVAL TIME.

foot-pad.

Here passes a man with two faces. His arms are neatly folded before, also behind. You cannot tell which is the real front, until, suddenly, a horse trots up and nearly touches noses, while the man moves on undisturbed. You meant to give that man a dash, but you forgot, he was so queer.

Ah! here comes a carriage of pretty girls. Down pours the shot from the balcony above. It rains on you like hail. It runs in rills down your back. You hold your recovered ears, and add your tone to the rippling, rippling laughter that flows on in silvery tide.

Not one boisterous shout, not one impatient excla-

"PROMENADE DU COURS" IN CARNIVAL TIME.

mation the whole livelong day; only everywhere the sound of childish glee. How good to see even old careworn faces lighted up with mirth!

Here goes an ostrich with a monkey on his back then a man with a whole suit of clothes neatly fitted out of Journals.

But — look! look! there towers a huge car. Nay,

it is a basket — a vegetable basket! but its sides are as high as our balcony. On its corners stand white carrots with their green waving tops upward. Around the edges are piled a variety of garden beauties.

But, wonderful to see, in the centre rises a mammoth cabbage. Its large-veined petals are as perfect as any you ever saw in your garden, but their tips reach above the third balcony. Upon these veined petals climb gorgeous butterflies, whose wings slowly shut and open while they sip. As the mammoth passes, the outer petals slowly droop, and snails are seen clinging within, while gayly-hued butterflies creep into view.

Now the carriages mingle gayly in the procession. Here is one with young lads, their faces protected with gauze masks, which laughably show shut red lips without, and two red lines of lips and white glittering teeth within. The battle of *confetti* waxes hot. Merry faces fill all balconies and windows. Many a beauty drops her mask for an instant like ourselves to peer more eagerly at the wonderful procession, but at her peril. On the instant *dash! dash!* flies the *confetti*, slung with force enough from the little scoops to sting sharply.

War is the fiercest yonder where there is such a

handsome family (Americans we are sure), father, mother and daughter.

Here goes a carriage decorated with United States flags; all its occupants cloaked and hooded in gray linen, the carriage covered likewise. They stop beneath the balcony, and *sling! sling! sling!* in wildest combat until crowded on.

Up and down the procession sweeps. Up one side the wide "*Cours*" and down the other; the space within filled with the merry surging crowd, under the feet of the horses it would seem. But no matter. Horses and men and women and children bear a charmed life to-day.

Now and then a policeman pounces on the boys, who are gathering up the heaps of *confetti* from the dirt to sell again; but this is the only suggestion of law and order behind the gay confusion.

Here rolls a carriage trimmed with red and white. Within are a pair of scarlet dominoes, who peer mysteriously at you.

But look again at what moves on. A car longer than any yet seen.

It is a grotto. Within its cool recesses bask immense lizards. Some slowly climb its sides, then, in search of prey, thrust out their long tongues. In shining coat, in color, in movement, you would avow them to be lizards, truly. But how huge!

Behind the lizards pass again the mounted grasshoppers, our favorites of all, for their wonderfully perfect form and dainty beauty. And lo! they bear, to our delight, a silken banner, token of the prize.

For, pets, do you read between the lines and understand that this wonderful procession was the result of truly artistic skill? — that to imitate perfectly to the eye, to represent exactly in motion all these living creatures, and yet conceal within a boy or man who invisibly moved them, required all the delicacy of perception and nicety of workmanship of French eyes and fingers? Think you that your little fingers and bright eyes will ever attain so much.

Besides, all this was also a great outlay of thousands of francs. For Nice aroused herself to excel in Carnival, and offered large prizes — one of five thousand francs, another of four, another of three — for the most perfect representations.

Nowhere in Italy was there anything to compare with Nice. And I doubt if you would see again in Carnival what would so perfectly delight your young eyes, or so quicken your perception of artistic skill.

We look at our watches. Two hours yet; but we long to taste the fun on foot. So we fling our last *confetti*, fill hair and button-holes and hands with our sweet nosegays of geranium, sweet alyssum, mignonette and pansies — mementoes of the fight, — then descend to the sidewalk to press our way along the crowded court.

More and more to see! and, last of all, Carnival tossed and tumbled in effigy until his death by drowning or burning.

But we must be early at the station. Early, indeed! Peppered and pelted all the way, tweaked and shot at; but ever and always with *only* the harmless *confetti* and soft nosegays.

Sure that we are the first to leave, sure that no others are there before us, we pass into the outer baggage-room. Fifty more are there pressed hard against the closed door.

The crowd swells; hundreds are behind us; we can scarcely keep our feet. Yet what a good-natured crowd! The hour for the train to leave passes. By and by the closed door opens a crack; a gilt-banded arm is thrust through and *one* person taken out, and the solemn door closed again.

So, one by one, we ooze through, pass the turnstile in the passage under surveillance of the keen-eyed officer, and are admitted into the saloon, which is also locked.

We sink down into a seat nearest *the* one of two doors which instinct tells us is to be opened. Again we wait an hour till the last panting victim is passed through the stile.

Then, O! it is not our door which unlocks and opens but the other. We rush for a compartment; but no! all appear filled, so we step to an official and state our case.

He conducts us on, on, nearly to the end of the train, over stones and timbers; but, at last, bestows us out of that crowd in a compartment with but three persons. Soon we leave, only two hours later than the time advertised.

For in France, little pets, the trains wait for the people. The people are locked in till all is ready; then follows a rush like a grand game of "puss, puss in the corner!" and almost always there is some poor puss who cannot get in.

Guess how many bushels of *confetti* rattled on the floor of our chamber that night!

ON THE FARM IN WINTER.

THE life of a boy in winter on the old-fashioned New England farm seems to me one of the best of the right kinds of life for a healthy lad, provided his tastes have not been spoiled by wrong reading, or by some misleading glimpse of a city by gas-light. It certainly abounds with the blood and muscle-making sports for which the city physiologists so anxiously strive to substitute rinks and gymnasiums.

But I rather pity a young fellow who gets his only sleigh rides by paying a dollar an hour to the livery-stable, and who must do his skating within limits on artificial ice. He never gets even a taste of such primitive fun as two boys I know had last winter. The sleigh was at the wagon-maker's shop for repairs when the first heavy snow fell, and they harnessed

Dobbin to an old boat, and had an uproarious ride up hill and down dale, with glorious bumps and jolts.

I rather pity a fellow, too, who eats grocer's apples, and confectioner's nuts, and baker's cream cakes, who never knows the fun of going down cellar to the apple bins to fill his pockets for school, and who owns no right in a pile of butternuts on the garret floor. I am sorry for a boy that knows nothing of the manly freedom of trowsers tucked in boots, hands and feet both cased in home-knit mittens and home-knit socks — I cannot believe his blood is as red, or can possibly flow so deep and strong in his sidewalk sort of life, as the young fellows who chop wood and ply the snow-shovel, and turn out *en masse* with snow-ploughs after a long storm — the sound of the future strength of the land is in the sturdy stamp of their snowy boots at the door as they come in from their hearty work. I am not writing of country boys that want to be clerks, — they are spoiled for fun anyhow, — but of the boys that expect, if they expect anything in particular, to stay on the farm and own it themselves some day.

This stinging cold morning the boys at the schoolhouse door are not discussing the play-bills of the *Globe* or the *Museum*, but how the river froze last night, turning the long quiet surface to blue-black ice, as smooth as a looking-glass. Now what skating! what grand noonings, what glorious evenings! No rink or frog-pond, where one no sooner gets under headway than he must turn about, but miles and miles of curving reaches leading him forward between rustling sedges, till he sees the white caps of the open lake dancing before him.

Presently the snow comes and puts an end to the sport; for sweeping miles and miles of ice is out of the question. After the snow, a thaw; and then the jolly snow-balling. There is not enough of a thaw to take the snow off; only enough to make it just sufficiently sloppy and soft for the freeze-up that follows to give it a crust almost as hard and smooth as the ice lately covered up.

Then such coasting! Just think of dragging your sled of a moonlight night up a mile of easy tramping to the foot of the mountain, whence you come down again, now fast, now slow, now "like a streak" down a sharp incline, now running over a

even-rail fence buried in the glittering drifts, and bringing up at last at a neighbor's door, or at the back side of your own barnyard!

It is great fun, too, to slide on the drifts with "slews" or "jump-ers." These are made sometimes of one, sometimes of two barrel-staves, and are sure to give you many a jolly bump and wintersault.

There is fun to be had *in* the drifts too, digging caves or under-snow houses, wherein you may build a fire without the least danger. Here you can be Esquimaux, and your whole tribe sally forth from the igloë and attack a terrible white bear, if one of the party will kindly consent to be a bear for awhile. You can make him white enough by pelting him with snow, and he will *bear* enough before he is finally killed.

There is fun, too, and of no mean order, to be got out of the regular farm duties. Not much, perhaps, out of bringing in the wood, or feeding the pigs, or turning the fanning-mill; but foddering the sheep and calves, which, very likely, are pets, takes the boys to the hay-mow, where odors of summer linger in the herds-grass, and the daisy and clover-tops are almost as green and white and yellow and purple as when they fell before the scythe.

What a place is this elastic floor for a "wrestle or a summersault!" and then, who "da's't" climb to the big beam, into the neighborhood of the empty swallows nests and dusty cobwebs, and take the flying jump therefrom to the mow? Here, too, are hens' nests to be found, with frost-cracked eggs to carry in rats, and larger prey, also to be hunted when the hay is so nearly spent that the fork sticks into the loose boards at the bottom of the hay.

But of all things which the farmer's boy is wanted to do, and wants to do, there is nothing such clear fun as the breaking of a yoke of calves. First, the little yoke is to be got on to the pair somehow and a rope made fast to the "nigh" one's head, that is, the calf on the left side, where the driver goes. Then comes bawling and hauling and pushing, and often too much beating, until the little cattle are made to understand that "Gee" means turn to the right, and "Haw" means turn to the left, and that "Whoa" means stop, and "Back" means, of them all, just what is said.

Every command is roared and shouted; for an

UPON THE HAY-MOW.

idea seems to prevail that oxen, big and little, are deaf as adders, and can never be made to hear except at the top of the voice. In a still, winter day, you may hear a grown-up ox-teamster roaring at his patient beasts two miles away; and a calf-breaker not half his size may be heard more than half as far. Then, on some frosty Saturday, when the little nubby-horned fellows have learned their lessons, they are hitched to a sled, and made to haul light loads, a little wood, or some of the boys,— the driver still holding to the rope, and flourishing his whip as grand as a drum-major.

Once in a while the little oxen of the future take matters into their own hoofs and make a strike for freedom, upsetting the sled and scattering its load, and dragging their driver headlong through the snow.

But they have to submit at last; and three or four years hence, you would never think from their solemn looks and sober pace that they ever had thought of such rebellious freaks. They were the boy's calves, but father's oxen.

Halter-breaking a colt is almost as good as breaking steers, only there is no sled-riding to be had in this.

ON THE FARM IN WINTER.

Till lately, the young fellow has had the freedom of the fields, digging in the first snows for a part of his living, and with his rough life has grown as shaggy-coated as a Shetland pony, with as many burrs stuck in his short foretop as it will hold; for if there is an overlooked burdock on all the farm, every one of the horse kind running at large will find it, and each get more than his share of burrs matted and twisted into his foretop and mane.

Now, he is waxed and driven into a shed or stable, and fooled or forced to put his head into a long, stout, rope halter. Then he is got into the clear, open meadow, and his first lesson begins. The boys all lay hold of the rope at a safe distance from the astonished pupil, and pull steadily upon him. Just now he would rather go any way than straight ahead, and holds back with all his might, looking, with all his legs braced forward, his neck stretched to its utmost, and his head on a line with it, like a stubborn little donkey who has lost something in ears, but nothing in willfulness, and gained a little in tail. At last he yields a little to the uncomfortable strain, and takes a few reluctant steps for-

BREAKING THE CALVES.

ward, then rears and plunges and throws himself, and is drawn struggling headlong through the snow, until he tires of such rough usage and flounders to his feet.

Then he repeats his bracing tactics, the boys bracing as stoutly against him, till he suddenly gives way and they go tumbling all in a heap.

If the boys tire out before the colt gives up, there are other days coming, and sooner or later he submits; and in part compensation for not having his own way, he has a warm stall in the barn, and eats from a manger, just like a big horse, and is petted and fondled, and grows to be great friends with his young masters — at last to be "father's horse," instead of "our colt."

But by and by the long winter — this play-day of the year for the farm-boy — comes to an end, to make way for spring — spring which brings to him work out of all reasonable proportion to the amount of play, at least so the farm-boy is likely to think.

A CHINAMAN'S QUEUE.

EVERYONE knows that a Chinaman wears his hair in a queue, but not every one knows why he does so. A Chinaman's queue is not a mere oddity or variety; it is, to him, a very serious thing; losing it, he would almost sell his respectability, and history tells of more than one time when it has been a matter of life and death.

In many of their customs the people of China follow their forefathers of more than a thousand years ago, but queues may be called a new fashion, having only been worn about two hundred and fifty years.

In very old times, the Chinese wore their long hair put up in a peculiar manner upon the tops of their heads, and called themselves "The Black-Haired Race;" but about the time that the Pilgrims landed at Plymouth, in the year 1627, the Tartars, who had come down from Manchuria, and, after long wars, had conquered China, which they have governed ever since, made a law that all the Chinese, to show that they had been conquered, should take down their top-knots, and wear their hair as the Tartars did, in a hanging braid; and they threatened to kill all who would not do it.

Of course the Chinese were greatly distressed by this; but, as it was better to have a tail than to be without a head, they submitted in the end, making the best of what they could not help.

The people of southern China held out longest against the queue, and, in one district, men were hired to wear it. Even now, dwelling among the hills, are a few men belonging to a very old and wild tribe, whose pride it is that they have never worn hanging hair; while the Amoy men, who were the very last to yield to the Tartars, wear a turban to hide the shaven head, and the detested tail; but some persons think that the nation in general have come to like the new style better that the old; others think that they would gladly go back to the old way, if they could.

A few years ago there was a great rebellion in China. A part of the Chinese rebelled against the Tartars, and all the rebels put up their hair in the old Chinese fashion; and, because they did not shave their heads, they went by the name of the "Long-Haired Robbers." When any of their soldiers met a man with a queue they knew that he was loyal to the Tartar government, and they would kill him, or cut off his queue, or do what they liked with him; and, on the other hand, the life of a "Long-Haired Robber" was not safe for a moment if he fell into the hands of the government troops. At length, after many, many millions of people were killed, queues carried the day, and the rebels were conquered.

I have heard that thieves sometimes have their queues cut off for a punishment, and, now and then, I suppose, a person's hair must fall off after illness, but, in these cases, it would grow again.

There are two classes of men in China who never wear queues — the Buddhist priests, who shave their heads all over, and who can be known by the color of their gowns, and their queer hats, and the Tauists, who, as a sign of their priesthood, wear their hair in a kind of twist on the back of their heads. With these few exceptions, every Chinaman has a queue, from the young child whose short hairs are pinched up, sometimes on the crown of the head, and sometimes on the sides of it, and braided with threads of red silk into a tight little tail a few inches long, so stiff that it stands straight out from the head, up to the almost bald old man, whose straggling gray hairs are tied into a thin wisp at the back of his neck.

The Chinese have usually a good quantity of hair, coarse, perfectly straight, and jetty black, except, in a few cases, where, from illness, the color is rusty black. They have hardly any beard, but some of them — though not often before they are grandfathers, and more than forty years old — wear a much-admired moustache. Accustomed to black locks and smooth faces, they look curiously on the full beards of the men, and the yellow curls of the children, of our fairer race, or, as they style us, "The Red-Headed Foreigners."

The Chinese shave the whole head, except a round patch on the crown, about as large as a breakfast saucer. On this they let the hair grow, and it is combed back and down, and tied firmly with a string, at the middle of the bottom of the patch. It is then divided into three strands and braided. If a man is very poor, he simply has a plat, the length of his hair, fastened at the end with a cotton string; but the Chinese have a good deal of pride about their hair, and, if they can afford it, like to have the queue handsomely made. Often tresses of false hair are added to it, for making which the hairs that fall out are carefully saved. Of course, the hair is thinner at the end than at the top, and to keep the braid of more even size, and to increase its length, long bunches of black silk cord are gradually woven into it.

Queues vary in length, but grown men often wear them hanging nearly to their shoes, the upper part of the braid being of hair, and the lower part of black silk cord, which is tied in a tassel at the end. In southern China, children's queues are made bright and jaunty with crimson silk.

For mourning white cord is used, and for half mourning blue. Also, persons in mourning do not have their heads shaven for a certain length of time. When the emperor dies, nobody in China is expected to be shaven for one hundred days.

Commonly, tidy, well-to-do people have their heads shaven every few days, and, as no one could easily shave the top of his own head, everybody employs a barber. Of course there are a great many barbers, and, with all the millions of people in China, they have a large business.

Besides the shops, many barbers have little movable stands containing all their tools, and they may often be seen plying their art by the wayside, or at the houses of their customers. The barber has a basin of hot water, a towel, and an awkward kind of razor; and when he has shaven and washed the head, and braided the hair of a man, he ends up all by patting him, with both hands, upon the back and shoulders, in a way which, to him, is truly delightful. For all this, his charge is not more than six cents, and a poor man would pay still less.

To make his queue thicker, sometimes a Chinaman wishes to grow more hair, and the barber will leave his head unshaven for, perhaps, a quarter of an inch all round the old circle of hair. When the new hair is an inch or two long, being very stiff, it stands up in a fringe — like a kind of black halo — all round his head, looking very comically, and annoying the Chinaman very much, until it is long enough to be put into the braid.

When a man is at work, he finds his queue very much in his way, and he binds it about his head, or winds it up in a ball behind, where he sometimes fastens it with a small wooden comb; but, in his own country, on all occasions of form and dress, he wears it hanging, and it would not be polite to do otherwise.

As it would take a long time to dry it, he dislikes to wet it, and, if rain comes on, hastens to roll it up and cover it.

Sometimes beggars, to make themselves look very wretched, do not dress their hair for a long time, and it becomes so frizzed and matted that hardly anything could be done to it, but to cut most of it off.

When a culprit is arrested in China, the officer takes hold of his queue and leads him to prison by it, often treating him very cruelly.

Little girls, as well as little boys, have their heads shaven when they are about a month old. This is done before an idol, with a good deal of parade. Young girls also wear their hair in queues, but as when older their heads are not shaven like those of the boys, a larger quantity of hair is drawn back into the braid, making it much heavier. When married their hair is put up in the fashion of the women of the district where they live, but married women never wear their hair braided.

One who has lived long in China does not like to see a thin, uneven queue, tied with a cotton string; it has a slovenly, poverty-stricken air; while a thick, glossy braid, with a heavy bunch of silk in the end of it, looks tidy and prosperous; and a neat plat of silvery hair betokens comfortable old age.

MEXICAN WATER-CARRIERS

A MEXICAN water-carrier is always an oddly-dressed fellow. He looks something like the man some one met "one misty, moisty morning," who was all clothed in leather. He has a leather cap, jacket and trousers, the last reaching only to his knees, and held aside with bright buttons of silver, so as to show the white cotton drawers beneath. Down the front of his jacket, too, and around the rim of his cap, are bright buttons. Fastened at his side is a leather wallet holding his money. On his feet are leather sandals. Over his head are two stout leather straps, holding two jugs of earthernware, one

Mexican Water-Carriers.

ALWAYS ON A LITTLE INDIAN TROT.

resting on his back and the other hanging in front.

He begins work early in the morning. If you go into any of the public squares in the city of Mexico, you will then see a great many of them all seated around the stone basin and busy preparing for the day's work. They reach far over the edge and, dipping up the water, fill their large jug. Throwing that on their backs they reach down once more and fill the smaller one, and then trot off and visit the different houses of the city, and sell the families what water they want.

You would say, perhaps, it was a heavy load to carry by the head and neck, but the carrier does not seem to mind it, for he is very strong, and the jugs just balance each other. It is said an Englishman was once told of this balance, and, to see if it were so, he waited until a carrier came along and then, with his cane, broke one of the jugs. Alas! down came the man, jugs and all; his balance surely was gone.

Water has to be brought about in this manner because none runs into the houses by lead pipes, as with us. It all comes from near the old castle of Chapultepec, three or four miles from the city.

It runs over great stone aqueducts, built by Cortes, and when it reaches the public square falls into the stone basins of the city. So, you see, it makes these carriers almost like our milkmen, only they do not come with a fine horse and carriage, and do not make nearly as much money. They only get a few cents each day. How hard they work, too! Busy from morn till eve, always earnest, hardly ever smiling, always on a little Indian trot, they go about from house to house, and then, when the day's work is over, what a life they lead!

They have no home to go to, either; they live in the streets, sleep in the gutter or on the cathedral stone steps, and often, I fear, get so befogged on "pulque," the national drink, that they care not whether they have a home and good bed or not.

Think what a miserable existence, not knowing how to read, dressing as those before them did three hundred years ago, and doing nothing but carrying water about the city. Every day they will go into the great cathedral and say their prayers. They put their jugs down beside them, clasp their hands, raise their eyes to the image of their patron saint, and mumble their requests or their thanks, and then, taking a last look at the gold candlesticks and rich ornaments, will hurry away, and continue their hard, uninteresting daily labors.

A VERY QUEER HOUSE.

THERE are few pleasanter places in summer than the great square of Et-Meidaun at Constantinople. The tall gray pointed monument in the middle, like a sentry watching over the whole place, the white houses along either side, the polished pavement, the high white walls and rounded domes, and tall slender towers and cool shadowy gateways of the Turkish mosques together with the bright blue sky overhead and the bright blue sea in the distance below, make a very pretty picture indeed.

The different people, too, that go past us are quite a show in themselves. Now, it is a Turkish soldier in blue frock and red cap — a fine tall fellow, but rather thin and pale, as if he did not always get enough to eat; now, a tall, dark, grave-looking American, with a high funnel-shaped hat, and a long black frock right down to his feet. There comes a big, jolly-looking English sailor, rolling himself along with his hands in his pockets and his hat on one side. There goes a Russian with a broad flat face and thick yellow beard. That tall handsome man in the laced jacket and black velvet trousers, who is looking after him so fiercely, is a Circassian, who was fighting against the Russians among the mountains of the Caucasus not many years ago. And behind him is an Arab water-carrier, with limbs bare to the knee and a huge skin bag full of water on his back.

But the strangest sight of all is still to come.

Halting to look around I suddenly espy a pair of yellow Turkish slippers, a good deal worn, lying at the foot of a huge tree which stands alone in the midst of the open space. They are not flung carelessly down, either, as if their owner had thrown them away, but placed neatly side by side; just as an orderly old gentleman might put *his* slippers beside the fire before going out. And, stranger still, although at least half a dozen bare-footed Turks (who might think even an old shoe worth picking up) have passed by and seen them, not one of them has ventured to disturb them in any way.

My Greek companion notices my surprise, and gives a knowing grin, like a man who has just asked you a riddle which he is sure you will never guess.

"Aha, Effendi! Don't you think he must have been a careless fellow who left his slippers there? See anything odd about this tree?"

"Nothing but that piece of board on it which I suppose covers a hollow."

"That's just it!" chuckles the Greek. "It covers a *hollow*, sure enough — look here, Effendi!"

He taps thrice upon the "piece of board," which suddenly swings back like a door, disclosing to my astonished eyes, in the dark hollow, the long blue robe, white turban, and flowing beard of an old Turk.

"Peace be with you!" says the old gentleman in a deep hoarse voice, nodding to my companion, whom he seems to know.

"With you be peace," answers the Greek. "You didn't expect that, did you, Effendi? It's not every day that you find a man living inside a tree?"

"*Does* he live here, then?"

"To be sure he does. Didn't you see his slippers at the door? Nobody would touch the slippers for any money. They all know old Selim. He has a snug house, after all; and don't pay *rent* either!"

In truth, the little place is snug enough, and certainly holds a good deal for its size. On one side is an earthen water-jar, on the other a huge blanket-like cloak, which probably represents Mr. Selim's whole stock of bedding. A copper stew-pan is fixed to a spike driven into the wood, while just above it a small iron funnel, neatly fitted into a knot-hole of the trunk, does duty as a chimney. Around the sides of the hollow hang a long pipe, a tobacco-pouch, a leathern wallet, and some other articles, all bearing marks of long service; while to crown all, my guide shows me, triumphantly, just outside the door, a wooden shelf with several pots of flowers — a garden that just matches the house.

Having given us this sight of his house-keeping, the old gentleman (who has been standing like a statue during the whole inspection) silently holds out his hand. I drop into it a double piastre (ten cents) and take my leave, reflecting that if it is good to be content with little this old hermit is certainly a bit of a hero in his way.

IN BELGIUM.

AFTER rolling and tossing for twenty-four hours upon the German Ocean, the sight of land should be hailed with a spirit of thankfulness. But of all inhospitable shores, those of the Belgian coast, in the month of November, must carry the palm. The waters, gray and rough, dash upon a sandy beach for miles and miles, showing no signs of life, if we except an occasional wind-mill in action. Row after row of poplar trees form a partial back-ground. Somewhat stripped of their leaves, they have the appearance of so many gray pillars holding up the sky.

As the low-built towns with their red houses rise to view, and the dikes present themselves, if this be the first introduction into Continental Europe, the foreignness stands out in bold relief. But as you ascend the river the villages are more interesting and indications of life more frequent. Long before reaching the pier at Antwerp, its towers salute the travellers, and the gratitude becomes apparent on each and every visage.

Our little windows in the above-mentioned city overlooked its prettiest park, in the centre of which stands the statue of Rubens. At the right, yet full in view, stands the Cathedral of Notre Dame, famous for its ninety-nine bells (why not one more?) and the masterpieces of the great artist of Antwerp.

Of these paintings, the "Assumption," which has within a comparatively short time been restored, is truly beautiful, the countenances of the several figures wearing a pure expression, which is not a characteristic of the Rubens face in general. The fame of the others is perhaps yet greater than that of the "Assumption," and everywhere in our own country are engravings and photographs of the same, on exhibition or in private collections. Before these the lover of art lingers to study, and studying continues to linger. For me, alas! these *chef d'œuvres*, "The Ascent to the Cross" and the "The Descent from the Cross," have no attractions.

The music of the bells at sunset repays one, not only for the tumble of the German Sea, but for the voyage across the Atlantic, especially in the autumn, when the twilights are so short that the Mall is lightest as the sun goes down. This music singularly contrasts with the noise made by the footfall of the peasants. This numerous class, hurrying home at dusk, take the park as their shorter course. The click-clack of the hundreds of wooden shoes of all sizes and intensities, rapidly "getting by," is something that can never be imagined. As these articles of apparel are seldom of a snug fit in the region of the heel, there is a peculiar introduction to each grand step. The quantity and quality of this noise are astonishing; the novelty, a charm.

There is one sound, however, which is sensibly wanting among the lower class of Belgians. It may never have been in the experience of others, but it could not be entirely my own imagination — I missed the human voice in the groups of peasantry. The uneducated of other countries have at least a common "mongrel tongue" to some extent, but the individual vocabulary of this class is certainly very limited, which is a check to prolonged conversation. This feature was to me a cause satisfactory for the stillness of the streets, thronged as they sometimes are, and may be the reason that the foot-fall is so impressive, with its wooden encumbrances.

In Belgium.

Next to the shoe, the attraction was the harnessed dogs and the young girls drawing burdens.

When a woman was seen wheeling a cart or trundling a barrow, it was just to conclude that she was in the interest of her own gain, and we could pass on. When the dogs, the old and despised of their kind, were leisurely carrying their wagon of vegetables, provided the driver was kind, it was rather a foreign sight than a painful one. Often these dogs lie down in the harness—the latter not being very elaborate — and do not seem unwilling to rise to the occasion. When it happened, as often it did, during our short sojourn in Belgium, that we saw girls, the young and bright and strong, bearing these burdens, frequently sharing the harness with the aforesaid animals, the American heart rebelled. If they were rough, hoydenish girls, romping all day long, filling their carts with sand for the fun and having a boy-companion as a play-driver, we should even then think, do they *never* go to school?

But they were not of this class! They were the quiet and obedient, generally tidy in appearance, calmly accepting their lot in life through ignorance. I never saw a boy thus disgraced; not that I feel less glad for "him," but the more sad for "her."

When walking one day, having lost my way, I met

one of these teams. There were connected with it two young girls, about fifteen years of age—one harnessed and drawing the load, the other having the charge of the cargo, which, from its too great abundance, required constant diligence. I inquired of them the direction to the hotel.

Without altering a muscle, they continued their gaze (we had begun the stare from afar). So listless was it that they seemed like pet animals, who look at one confidingly, except in the case of the latter there will be "wink of recognition." No attempt was made to reply. After I turned, they kept their eyes upon the space which I had occupied, as if I had merely been an obstruction to their sunshine. A person, not far from them, answered my inquiries, adding, with a nod towards the "little workers," "they only talk mongrel."

This woman, short and chubby, forcibly reminded me of somebody or something in the past. After a brief reflection, behold the solution:

Before toys had become so elaborate in our own country, there occasionally found their way from Holland images of pewter, representing the dairymaids of that part of Europe. They were far different from the pewter-pieces of the present day, being thicker and less destructible. The one that came into my possession, the delight of my heart, wore the short, full dress and sun-bonnet, with arms akimbo. The one, ah me! that would have been my choice was purchased by a class-mate, she having at that time, and I presume at this time, twice my amount of funds. The price of this precious bit was two cents.

The latter figure, unlike mine, had the pail poised upon the head. It was probably a true likeness of the renowned maid that counted the chickens in advance, thereby showing the people of her country to have been "born calculators.' I think the little body that showed me the way to my lodgings descended in a direct line from this old mathematical stock, and was a little proud of her origin. Her language was a mixture of Dutch, French, and, for all I know, several dead languages, *but* — and I have her own authority for it — not a mongrel tongue. Out of gratitude to one who led me to my home, I should speak well of this woman, as of the proverbial bridge, so am quite willing to accept her statement and allow her a "pure dialect."

JOE THE CHIMPANZEE.

WHEN in England I was very much interested in the monkeys at the Zoological Gardens, Regent's Park, London. There were hundreds of all kinds and sizes, from the gigantic orang-outang to tiny creatures not much bigger than a large rat.

These monkeys had a spacious glass house, heated by steam; and as a tropical temperature was always maintained, tall palms and luxurious vines grew so vigorously within its walls that I have no doubt the quaint inmates supposed themselves in their native haunts.

They chattered and scolded each other, wildly chased stray little dogs and kittens, and really seemed to know so much that I half believed an old keeper, who told me the only reason they did not talk, was because they could make themselves well enough understood without.

Many funny stories I heard of their sagacity. One I recall of a nurse who shook a naughty little boy in the presence of some of the mother monkeys, whereupon all the old monkeys began shaking all the young ones until it seemed as if their poor little heads would drop off.

But, interested in all the singular inhabitants of the house, I grew attached to Joe, the young chimpanzee who had been brought a baby from the coast of Guinea the winter before. He had a little room on the sunny side of the monkey house, with a stove, table, chairs and a couple of beds arranged like the berths in the state room of an ocean steamer. Besides he had a man all to himself, to wait upon him; and it was no wonder the other monkeys were jealous of his superior quarters and the deference paid him; for while Joe was not handsome he was worth more money than all the others put together.

He was worth this great sum because he belonged to the most intelligent and interesting species of the monkey family, and only one or two of his kinsfolk had ever been seen in Europe, while the only one the Zoological Society had ever owned, had died of lung fever before he had inhabited his comfortable quarters many months.

Joe was about as tall as an average boy of eight or ten years. He wore a thick cloth roundabout, and a low flat trencher cap such as the Oxford students delight in.

One day I walked to the door of his room and knocked. The keeper said "Come in," and as I did so Joe walked erect over the floor to me, pulled off his cap with his left hand, and put out his right to shake mine. When I said "It is a fine morning," he bowed briskly; but when I added, "Are you pretty well, Joe?" he shook his head and looked very sober. The keeper explained: "Joe had a cold, and that made him very low spirited."

Joe was listening attentively; and when the man finished, he shivered and drew up the collar of his jacket round his hairy throat, as if to confirm the statement.

I gave him an apple, which he looked at a moment, then opened the door of the oven of his stove, and put it in out of sight. Seeming to understand that the fire was low, he pulled a basket from under the lower berth and took some bits of wood from it to the stove. Then the keeper handed him a match, and he lighted a fire as cleverly as any Yankee boy I ever saw.

"Show the lady how you read *The Times*, Joe," said the keeper.

JOE READS "*The Times.*"

Joe drew up a chair, tilted it back a little, spread his legs apart, opened the sheet, turned it until he found the page he wanted, then settled himself into the exact position of the comfortable English gentle-

Joe the Chimpanzee.

man who supposes *The Times* is printed for his exclusive use. It was impossible to help laughing, and the sly twinkle in his narrow eye assured us Joe himself knew how funny it was.

Quite a crowd had gathered at the open door of his room, and as he noticed it, he put his hand in his pocket drew out the one eye-glass Englishman so particularly affect, and put it to his eye looking as weakly wise as Lord Dundreary himself. After a little he grew tired of so many spectators, left his chair and quietly shut the door in their faces.

Looking about as if he would do something more for our amusement, he remembered his apple in the stove oven. Running there he took hold of the door, but suddenly drew back, for it was hot. He laughed a little at his discomfiture which he took in good part, stood thinking a moment, then used his pocket-handkerchief as deftly as a dainty lady would to accomplish his purpose. But if the door was hot, the apple, Joe logically reasoned, must be hotter; so he ventured not to touch it before opening his knife. Wondering what he was going to do, I found him sticking the blade into the apple and bringing it out in triumph. The keeper gave him a plate, and after letting the apple cool a little he offered it to us. We courteously declined, but the servant tasted, explaining that Joe did not like to eat anything alone. Then Joe followed, but did not like the flavor, and being asked if it was sour, he nodded. We were

JOE TRIES HIS APPLE.

told that he, in common with the other monkeys, liked oranges and bananas better than any other fruits.

Yet he kept tasting a little of the apple from a spoon while the keeper told us how the sailors who hoped to capture his mother only succeeded in bringing him off alive after they had killed her. They had hard work to keep him alive on board ship, but found a warm nook for him by the galley fire. He was in fair health when they landed, so they obtained the large price offered by the Zoological Gardens; but in spite of the most devoted care, he seemed to languish in his new home.

"Do you love me, Joe?" the man ended his story with. Joe nodded, smiled, and put his head lovingly on the other's shoulder.

As we left that day, Joe took his hat, cane, and heavy wrap, and escorted us to the great door of the monkey house, shaking our hands as we bade him good-bye.

Another time when I called he was taking tea, using milk and sugar and handling cup and saucer as if he had been familiar with them from his earliest days. He motioned us to take chairs. We did so and he jumped up, found cups for us, and then passed a plate of biscuits, laughing with glee as we took one. I have taken tea with many curious individuals, but never expect to be so honored again as to be invited by a chimpanzee.

Noticing his hand was feverish, I found his pulse was 130. I said "What is the matter of him?"

"Consumption is what kills all of them," the man answered, low, just as if talking before a human invalid.

From that day Joe failed rapidly, and one morning under the head of "Great Loss," *The Times* announced that he died at midnight.

I went down at once to see the keeper whose grief I knew would be keen.

He told me how for days, Joe could only be persuaded to take food by seeing him eat and hearing him praise it, how he made him sleep in his berth by his side, and when death came, held his hand through all the last struggle.

The man's voice was actually choked with sobs as he said, "It don't seem right, indeed it don't, not to have a funeral for him! He ought to have had it."

I never heard Joe had any funeral, but I did hear that he was stuffed, and looks more like a big boy than when he was alive.

MARKET DAY AT PAU.

IF you don't know where Pau is, do as I did when I first heard of it, — look it up on some large map of France.

Down in the southeast corner, at the mouth of the Adour river, you will see the city from which the bayonet is said to have received its name; and if you move your finger along about an inch due east from Bayonne you will be likely to pass it directly under Pau.

It is the capital of one of the finest departments of France, the Basses-Pyrenees; and its mild, equable climate and charming scenery have made it, for the last thirty years, a favorite winter resort for invalids and pleasure-seekers.

As the capital of the old province of Béarn, and as the seat of the ancient royal castle where flourished the Gastons and Marguerites, and where Henri IV. of France was born, Pau has many interesting historical associations, upon which, however, we must resolutely turn our backs if we mean to go to market this morning.

Monday is always market-day at Pau, and then it is that the country comes bodily in and takes possession of the town. At five o'clock in the morning the rumbling of cart-wheels and the clatter of sabots down in the cold gray streets announce the approach of a rustic army from the villages round about. On they come from every quarter all through the forenoon, and if we walk out anywhere — say to the Alléés de Morlaäs, where we can sit on one of the benches under the trees and gaze now and then at the distant snowy Pyrenees, — we shall see the endless stream of market-people.

The men wear round woolen caps without visors, called the *béret*; a short frock, usually of some coarse cotton material, which is gathered so much about the neck as not to improve their stumpy figures; and huge wooden shoes that rattle and thump along the pavements, bringing with them on rainy days an incredible quantity of country mud.

The most noticeable feature in the dress of the women is the bright foulard handkerchief that serves instead of hat or bonnet. It is arranged according to the taste and age of the wearer, and is capable of producing a wide range of effects.

The guide-book assures us that the *paysannes* walk

A PEASANT WOMAN.

barefoot on the country roads; but, upon approaching the town, they cover their wayworn feet with the cherished shoes and stockings that have thus been spared from wear and tear.

On a cold spring morning we saw a company of women descending a hill at Lourdes with enormous bundles of wood on their heads. As we were pitying the bare feet that went toiling down the steep way, we suddenly spied their shoes dangling from the fagots where they had considerately placed them, to be out of harm.

The strength of these little peasant women is wonderful. They walk off with grand strides, carrying heavy burdens on their heads, and sometimes knitting as they go. Many of the young girls are very pretty; but exposure and hard work soon change the fresh tint and the graceful outlines to a brown wrinkled visage and a gaunt ungainly figure.

Sitting here, we are attracted by a jaunty young creature tripping along with a large, round, shallow basket of salad, or *choux de Bruxelles*, on her head, carelessly steadying it with one hand, while in the other she carries a pair of chickens or a basket of eggs. But how can we see a pinched-looking woman tugging along under a big bag of potatoes, or breaking stones on the road, without feeling tired ourselves and sad? And neither the sadness nor the weariness is lightened upon seeing, as we invariably do, that when a woman is working with a man he generously gives her the heaviest end of the load.

The wood is brought in on clumsy carts, generally two-wheeled and often covered. The oxen and cows that draw these carts have their bodies draped with coarse linen covers, and across their heads is a strip of sheep-skin, which is worn with the shaggy side out

OX-TEAM.

and the skinny side in. M. Taine tells us in his book on the Pyrenees that he saw the heads of the cattle protected by thread nets and ferns, which, I trust is their usual summer coiffure; for in a country where, in winter, gentlemen carry parasols and wear large white streamers depending from their hats, to protect the head and back of the neck from the too ardent rays of the sun, even the " patient ox " might complain of the unfitness of a head-dress of sheep skin.

The driver of the ox-team is armed with a long stick, at the end of which is an iron goad. This he uses either in guiding the cattle, which is done by going in advance of them and stretching the stick backward with a queer, stiff gesture, or in pricking and prodding the poor creatures till they hardly know which way to turn. The cattle, which are mostly of a light brown color, are very large and fine; but it seems strange to us to see cows wearing the yoke.

But, O! the donkey! The wise, the tough, the musical, the irresistible, the universal donkey! How shall I ever give you an idea of what he becomes to an appreciative mind that has daily opportunities of studying his "tricks and manners!"

Fancy one of these long-eared, solemn-eyed gentry, scarcely larger than a good-sized Newfoundland dog jogging along with a double pannier bulging at his sides and a fat market-woman on his back.

But the disproportion between the size of the beast and that of his burden, and his gravity and circumspection, is scarcely funnier here than when he is placed before a two-wheeled cart, a story and a half higher than himself, and containing a man, a woman, a boy, and a pig; sometimes cabbages and chickens, often two or three inexperienced calves. And in the afternoon, when market is over, I have often seen six or seven women huddled into one of these primitive chariots, each provided with the inevitable stocking

"One of these long-eared, solemn-eyed gentry."

her tongue and her knitting-needles keeping time as the cart goes tilting along over the famous roads of the Basses-Pyrénées. The gay handkerchiefs of the women, the purple, blue and gray stockings with their flashing needles, and the huge brown loaves of bread sure to be protruding in various quarters, made these groups, returning from market, most picturesquely striking.

Coming in from the *Allées de Morlaäs* we find, as we approach the *Place des Ecoles*, an animated scene. The broad sidewalk is lined with rows of women selling vegetables, fruit, flowers, poultry and eggs. The haggling of the buyers and the gibing of the venders, though carried on in *patois* unintelligible to us, are expressed in tones and accompanied by gestures that translate them quite effectively; especially as not a market-day passes without a long recital from our Catherine, illustrating the greed of the peasants and her own superior finesse.

"How much do you want for this chicken?"

"Three francs."

"Keep your chicken for somebody see. I'll go to another."

"Stay! What will you give for it?"

"Two francs."

"Get along with you!"

As Catherine eyes the chicken which she secretly admires and openly abuses, another cook comes up and lays her hand on its comely breast. It is a decisive moment, but Catherine is equal to the emergency.

"Stand off there! I'm here first."

Then, with a secret resolve that her *demoiselles* shall dine on that little plump *poulet*, she offers fifty sous and carries off the prize. To see her enter our *salon* bearing a waiter on which are a dozen fine rosy apples and two large russet pears, with the question, "Guess how much I paid for all?" written in every line of her shrewd old face, is something worth coming to Europe for. To make a sharp bargain, to cook a good dinner, and never to waste anything, these are the aims of her life and the themes of her discourse.

Our snug *appartement* is opposite the *Place des Ecoles*, where the wood and cattle are sold; and the first peep in the morning gives us a picture, lively enough and foreign enough to make us look and look again many times during the day, till late in the afternoon when the *Place* is nearly bare; and the aspect of the few patient but rather dejected-looking peasants whose wood has not yet found purchasers almost tempts us to run over and buy a load or two, just for the pleasure of sending the poor creatures home with lighter hearts and heavier pockets. What would Catherine say to that, I wonder?

Besides the interest which we feel in the various natural hangers-on of the wood-carts (and each one has from two to five of both sexes and all sizes), we

Market-Day at Pau.

"The favorite way of transporting a pig."

get no small amusement from their patrons, who represent all sorts of townspeople, from the fat old woman of the green grocery and sausage-shop over the way, who peddles with easy affability among the market-people, to the lordly young Englishman who dashes on to the *Place* with the air of a conquering hero, and loftily indicates with his riding-whip the load that has the honor to meet his approval.

Troops of frisky calves are scattered about, and groups of blue blouses and red *bérets* are earnestly discussing the merits of the unsuspecting innocents. More rarely a fine cow, or a yoke of oxen, attracts a circle of connoisseurs; then the *patois* becomes more fluent, and the gestures more animated, and the fists of the interested parties are seen flourishing unpleasantly near the disdainful noses of the critics.

The prolonged and penetrating squeal of that pig in the *Rue des Cultivateurs* reminds me that this interesting animal figures largely in the scenes of market-day. Pork being an important article of peasant diet, Mr. Piggy is always abroad on Monday and contributes largely to the general éclat.

The favorite way of transporting a moderate sized pig is to put him about the neck, holding his hind feet with one hand and his forefeet with the other. This method, though attended with some disadvantages, such as the proximity of the squeal to the ear of the carrier, is, on the whole, less worrying than that of tying a string to one of the hind legs of his Porkship, this giving him a chance to pull his way with more or less effect, while the peasant is frantically jerking in the opposite direction.

Not infrequently a pig gets a ride home from market in the cart of his new owner. Then, true to his nature and principles, he resists the honor accorded him with the whole might of his legs and lungs; so that, with a man at his hind legs, a woman at his left ear, and a boy at his right fore leg, he is with difficulty assisted to his coach and is held there, *en route*, by that "eternal vigilance" which is, in more senses than one, "the price of liberty."

On the *Rue Porte Neuve* and near the *Halle Neuve*, in the centre of the town, the venders of agricultural implements, kitchen hardware, locks and keys, second-

"A GRAY-HAIRED SPINNER WITH HER ANCIENT DISTAFF."

hand books, handkerchiefs, collars, cuffs, hats, bracelets, rings, baskets. brooms, bottles, mouse-traps, and other miscellaneous articles, display their goods, and a sudden shower makes bad work in this busy community.

Market-Day at Pau.

By the *Halle Neuve* is the fruit and vegetable market also, and farther on, in the *Rue de la Préfecture*, we suddenly come upon a hollow square inclosed on three sides by ancient looking buildings, one of which is the *Nieille Halle*; and here are fish, poultry and game, and the queerest-looking market-people in the whole town, it seems to me.

There is a flower market on the *Place Royal*, and you will see the Spanish women there, with their foulards and trinkets, to catch a few sous from the rustics.

We cannot confine our interest to the market-folk, however, for everybody is more or less picturesque in this strange land, and we are never tired of saying, "See here," and "See there." Sometimes it is a gray-haired spinner with her ancient distaff that attracts our notice, as she sits in a sunny door-way or totters along the sidewalk; and then there are the antics of these foreign children! Béarnais boys are as fond of standing on their heads as their American brethren are, but their large and heavy *sabots* are a great inconvenience.

Just look at those wooden shoes ranged along the sidewalk over there, while the owners thereof are flourishing their emancipated heels in fine style.

These are some of the sights of a market-day at

Pau; but how can you ever get a notion of the sounds? For when we add to the market-day hubbub the various every-day street cries that mingle

"As fond of standing on their heads as their American brethren."

with it we have a strange orchestra.

There are the charcoal men, who begin on a high key and drop with an almost impossible interval to a prolonged, nasal, twanging note; the old clo' men, whose *patois* for rags sounds so exactly like my companion's name that she is sure they are after the dresses she is economically wearing out at Pau; the chimney-sweeps; the *jonchée* women, who sell cream cheese, rolled in what looks like onion-tops; the roasted chestnut women, whose shrill "Tookow!" (*patois* for "*Tout chaud*") suggests piping-hot chestnuts in bursting shells; and the crockery and earthen men, who push their wares before them in long shallow box-carts, and give, in a sustained recitative, the whole catalogue of delf and pottery.

In the afternoon when the noise and stir are subsiding, we hear a few notes, often repeated, from what I should like to call a shepherd's pipe; only the instrument in question is not in the least like one, but resembles more one of those little musical toys with a row of holes cut along one side, upon which our children at home are so fond of performing. However, our shepherd contrives to produce a pastoral effect with his simple strain, and we favor the illusion of the pipe by only listening to him, while we look at his pretty goats with long, silky black hair. He leads them through the town twice a day, and at the sound of his call those who wish goat's milk send out their glasses and get it warm from a goat milked at the door. As his last faint notes die out in the distance the rosy light fades from the peaks of the Pyrenees; the sun has set, and market-day is over.

IL SANTISSIMO BAMBINO.

ON the Capitoline Hill, in Rome, stands a church, twelve hundred years old, called Ara Cœli. It is unpromising in its outward appearance, but is rich in marbles and mosaics within.

The most precious possession of this ancient church however, is a wooden doll called Il Santissimo Bambino — The Most Holy Infant. It is dressed like an Italian baby, and an Italian baby is dressed like a mummy. We often see them in their mothers' arms, so swathed that they can no more move than a bundle without any baby inside of it. Their little legs must ache for the freedom of kicking. The dress of *the* Bambino is very different from that of *a* bambino after all, for it is cloth of silver, and it sparkles all over with jewels which have been presented to it, and it wears a golden crown upon its head.

This is the history of this remarkable doll, as devout

THE BAMBINO. Page 205.

Roman Catholics believe. You must judge for yourselves how much of it is truth and how much fable.

They say this image of the infant Saviour was carved from olive-wood which grew upon the Mount of Olives, by a monk who lived in Palestine; and, as he had no means of painting it with sufficient beauty, his prayers prevailed upon St. Luke to come down from Heaven and color it for him. Then he sent it to Rome to be present at the Christmas festival. It was shipwrecked on the way, but finally came safely to land, and was received with great reverence by the Franciscan monks, who placed it in a shrine at Ara Cœli. It was soon found to have miraculous power to heal the sick, and was so often sent for to visit them, that, at one time, it received more fees than any physician in Rome. It has its own carriage in which it rides abroad, and its own attendants who guard it with the utmost care.

One woman was so selfish as to think it would be a capital thing if she could get possession of this wonder-working image for herself and her friends.

"She had another doll prepared of the same size and appearance as the 'Santissimo,' and having feigned sickness and obtained permission to have it left with her, she dressed the false image in its clothes, and sent it back to Ara Cœli. The fraud was not discovered till night, when the Franciscan monks were awakened by the most furious ringing of bells and by thundering knocks at the west door of the church, and, hastening thither, could see nothing but a wee, naked, pink foot peeping in from under the door; but when they opened the door, without stood the little naked figure of the true Bambino of Ara Cœli, shivering in the wind and rain. So the false baby was sent back in disgrace, and the real baby restored to its home, never to be trusted away alone any more."

This marvelous escape is duly recorded in the Sacristy of the church where the Bambino safely dwells under lock and key all the year, except the time from Christmas to Epiphany, when it comes out to receive the homage of the people.

We went to see it last Christmas.

As I told you, the church stands on one of the Seven Hills of the Eternal City; it is approached by a flight of stone steps as wide as the building itself and as high as the hill. There were many beggars on these steps; some old and blind, others young and bright-eyed. Beside the beggars, there were people with tiny images of the Baby in the Manger, toy sheep, and pictures of the Bambino for sale.

When we went into the church, we found one of the

THE EQUIPAGE OF THE BAMBINO.

chapels fitted up like a tableau. The chapels are something like large alcoves along the sides of a church. Each is consecrated to some saint, and often belongs to some particular family who have their weddings and funerals there.

It was in the second chapel on the left that we found the scene represented. The Virgin Mary was dressed in a bright blue silk, adorned with various jewels. In her lap lay the Bambino, about the size of a baby six weeks old. I do not believe St. Luke painted its face, for it was not half so well done as most of the wooden dolls we see. An artificial mule had his nose close to the baby's head. Joseph sat near, and in front the shepherds were kneeling. All these people were of life-size, made of wood, and dressed in real clothes. Beyond them was to be seen a pretty landscape — sheep, covered with real wool, a girl with a pitcher on her head coming down a path to a sparkling fountain of *glass*. In the distance was the town of Bethlehem. In mid-air hovered an angel, hung by a wire in his back from the ceiling. On pasteboard screens, above the Virgin and Child were painted a crowd of cherubs looking down, and in their midst God the Father — whom no one hath seen nor can see — was represented in the likeness of a venerable man, spreading his hands in blessing over the group below.

Il Santissimo Banbino.

A great many little children were coming with the older people to look at all this, and talking, in their pretty Italian tongue, about the "Bambino."

Epiphany, as perhaps you know, is the day kept in memory of the visit of the Wise Men where the Star in the East guided to our Saviour's cradle. On that day, Il Santissimo Bambino was to be carried with all ceremony back to the Sacristy; so we went to see that.

We were glad to find the Blessed Virgin had two nice silk dresses; she had changed from blue to red, and the Bambino was standing on her knee. The Shepherds had gone, and the Wise Men had come, all very gorgeous in flowered brocade and cloth of gold, with crowns on their heads, and pages to hold their trains.

It was yet an hour or two before the "Procession of the Bambino" would proceed; so we went out of the side door of the church to stray about the Capitoline Hill in the meanwhile.

We went down the steps where Tiberias Gracchus, the friend of the people, was killed, some two thousand years ago. That brought us into a small square called Piazza di Campidoglio. It is surrounded on three sides by public buildings, and in front has a grand stairway leading down to the street. It was in this very spot that Brutus made his famous speech after the assassination of Julius Cæsar. We crossed the square, went up some steps and through an arch-way.

A company of little Romans were playing soldier there, and the small drum-major made the walls of the capitol resound with his rattling music. That reminds me to tell you that Santa Claus does not visit Italy; but an old woman, named Navona, comes instead. She may be his wife, for aught I know; in fact, it seems quite likely, for she has a way, just like his, of coming down the chimney, bringing gifts for the good children and switches for the naughty. These must have been very good little boys, for every one of them seemed to have a new sword or gun. Probably Navona has to keep the house while Santa Claus is away about his Christmas business, and that is the reason she does not reach her small people here until the night before Epiphany, the 6th of January.

We went down a lane of poor houses, dodging the clothes which hung drying over our heads, and came to a large green gate in the high stone wall of a garden. We knocked, but no one answered. Presently a black-eyed little boy came running to us, glad to earn two or three sous by going to call the *custode*. While we wait for him to do so, I must tell you why we wished to go through this green door. You have read, either in Latin or English, the story of Tarpæia, the Roman maiden, who consented to show the Latin soldiers the way into the citadel if they would give her what they wore on their left arms, meaning their bracelets, and then the grim joke they played after she had done her part, by throwing upon her their shields, which were also "what they wore on their left arms."

It was to see the Tarpæian rock, where she led her country's enemies up, and where, later, traitors were hurled down, that we wished to go through the gate. Presently the keeper came, a rosy young woman, leading a little girl, who was feeling very rich over a new dolly she was dangling by its arm.

We were admitted to a small garden, where pretty pink roses were in blossom, and the oranges were hanging on the trees, though the icicles were fringing the fountain not far away. On the edge of the garden, along the brow of the cliff, runs a thick wall of brown stone; we leaned over it and looked down the steep rock which one assaulting party after another tried, in old times, to scale.

It was on this side that the Gauls were trying to reach the citadel at the time the geese saved the city Do you know that for a long time, annually, a dog

FAMILY OF ROMAN BEGGARS.

was crucified on the capitol, and a goose carried in triumph, because, on that occasion, the dogs failed to give the alarm and the geese did it!

We looked down on the roofs and into the courts of poor houses which have huddled close about the foot of the hill, but beyond them we could look down into the Forum, where Virginia was stabbed, where Horatius hung up the spoil of the Curiatii, where the body of Julius Cæsar was burned, where the head of Cicero was cruelly exposed on the very rostrum where had often been seen the triumph of his eloquence. Opposite to us stood the Palatine Hill, a mass of crumbling palaces; a little farther off rose the mighty wall of the Coliseum, where the gladiators used to fight, and where so many Christian martyrs were thrown to the wild beasts while tens of thousands of their fellow-men, more cruel than lions, looked on, for sport.

Just at the roots of the Capitoline, close by, though out of sight, was the Mamertine Prison, where St. Paul, of whom the world was not worthy, was once shut up in the dismal darkness of the dungeon.

As we went from the garden back to the Piazza di Campidoglio, we saw something unusual was going on in the palace on the left of the capital. In the door stood a guard in resplendent array of crimson and gold lace. Looking through the arched entrance, we could see in the inner court an open carriage with driver and footman in livery of bright scarlet. Something of a crowd was gathering in the corridors. We stopped to learn what it was all about. An Italian woman answered, "La Principessa Margarita!" and an English lady close by explained that the Princess Margaret, wife of the crown prince, had come to distribute prizes to the children of the public schools. Only invited guests could be present, but the people were waiting to see her come down. So we joined the people and waited also.

It was a long time and a pretty cold one. A brass band in the court cheered our spirits now and then. The fine span of the princess looked rather excited, at first, by the trumpets so close to their ears, but they stood their ground bravely. If one of the scarlet footmen tightened a buckle, it raised our hopes that his mistress was coming; the other put a fresh cigar in his mouth, and they sank.

Meantime the guard in the gold-laced crimson coat and yellow silk stockings paced up and down. At length there was a messenger from above; the royal carriage drove under the arch close to us. There was a rustle, and down came the princely lady, dressed in purple velvet, with mauve feathers in her hat, a white veil drawn over her face, and a large bouquet in her white-gloved hand — rather pretty, and very graceful. Before entering her carriage, she turned to shake hands with the ladies and gentlemen who had accompanied her. She was very complaisant, bowing low to them, and they still lower to her. Then she bowed graciously to the crowd right and left, and they responded gratefully. She smiled upon them, high and low, but there was a look in her face, as it passed close to me, as if she was tired of smiling for the public. She seated herself in the carriage; the lady-in-waiting took her place beside her, the gentleman-in-waiting threw over them the carriage-robe of white ermine lined with light blue velvet and stepped in himself.

Then the equipage rolled off, the scarlet footmen getting up behind as it started. This princess is very good and kind, greatly beloved by the people, and, as there is no queen, she is the first lady in the kingdom. Her husband first and her little son next are heirs to the crown.

This show being over, we hastened back to the church, fearing we had missed the Bambino in our pursuit of the princess. But we were in good time. On the side of the church opposite the tableau was a small, temporary platform. Little boys and girls were placed upon this, one after the other, to speak short pieces or recite verses about the Infant Christ. It was a kind of Sunday-school concert in Italian. The language is very sweet in a child's mouth. There were a great many bright, black-eyed children in the church, and most of them seemed to have brought their Christmas presents along with them, as if to show them to the Bambino.

There were ragged men in the crowd, and monks, and country-women with handkerchiefs tied over their heads for bonnets. One of them who stood near me had her first finger covered with rings up to the last joint. That is their great ambition in the way of dress.

At length the organ ceased playing, and the notes of a military band were heard. Then we saw a banner moving slowly down one of the aisles, followed by a train of lighted tapers. Over the heads of the people we could only see the banner and the lights; they passed down and paused to take the Bambino. Then they marched slowly all around the church — people falling on their knees as they passed by.

Out at the front door they went, and that sacred image was held high aloft, so that all the people on the great stairway and in the square below might get a sight of it, and be blessed. Then up the middle of the church they came, to the high altar. This was our chance to see them perfectly.

First the banner with the image of the Virgin on it

was borne by a young priest dressed in a long black robe and a white short gown trimmed with lace; next came a long procession of men in ordinary dress, carrying long and large wax candles, which they had a disagreeable habit of dripping as they went along.

"Servants of great houses," remarked a lady behind me.

"They used to come themselves," answered another.

Then followed Franciscan monks in their brown copes, each with a knotted rope for a girdle, and sandals only on his bare feet. After these came the band of musicians, all little boys; and now approached, with measured tread, three priests in rich robes of white brocade, enriched with silver. The middle one, a tall, venerable-looking man, with hoary hair and solemn countenance, held erect in his hands the sacred dolly. As it passed, believers dropped upon their knees. When he reached the high altar, he reverently kissed its feet, and delivered it to its custodian to be carried to the Sacristy!

CHILDREN UNDER THE SNOW.

F AR away up in the north, on the shores of that great frozen ocean lying beyond Europe and Asia, you may sometimes catch sight (as I did once) of a huge, gray, pointed thing, standing all alone in the midst of the snowy plain, just like an immense pear with the stalk upward. I should have been puzzled had I not seen a thin curl of smoke creeping from the top of it; but *that* let me into the secret. This queer-looking thing was a Samoiede tent!

The tent of a Samoiede is almost as simple an affair as that of an Arab. All you have to do is to plant a dozen long poles in the ground, slanted so as to let their tops meet; cover this framework with reindeer skins, leaving a hole at the top to let out the smoke; pile the snow high up around the lower part to keep off the wind—the "house" is complete.

But, outlandish as it looks, this little burrow is worth something in a real Russian frost, which freezes the very breath on one's moustache; so I go right up to the *door*, (which is simply a thick skin hanging over a hole in the side,) lift it, and step in.

The inside is certainly warm enough — rather too warm, in fact, being almost as hot and choky as a bake-house. There is a fire burning in the middle, the smoke going anywhere and everywhere; and beside it sat three things, (one can hardly call them human figures) one a deal larger than the other two.

There being no light but the glare of the fire, it is not easy for me to see where I am going; and the first thing I do is to stumble over something which seems like a skin bag, unusually full. But it is not — it is a *child*, wrapped or rather tied up in a huge cloak of deer-skin, and rolling about the floor like a ball.

In these out-of-the-way places, where a man may go for days without seeing a human face except his own, people call upon each other without waiting to be introduced; and my sudden entrance does not seem to disturb my new friends in the least. They greet me cordially enough, and bid me welcome in Russian, which most of the Samoiedes speak a little; and, seating myself on a chest, I look about me.

As my eyes get used to the half-light, I see that the

group by the fire consists of a woman and two little girls, muffled in skins from head to foot. Papa is away somewhere with his sledge and his reindeer, leaving mamma to mind the house and take care of the children. Funny little things they are, with great round heads, and dark-brown skins, and small, restless black eyes, and faces as flat as if somebody had sat down upon them; but, queer as they look, they have learned to make themselves useful already, for they are hard at work stitching their own clothes. They are not a bit shy, and in another minute I have them scrambling up into my lap, and wondering at the ticking of my watch, which I take out to show them, while they clap their hands and shout "*Pai, pai!*" which is their word for "good."

The tent is not a very large one, but every inch of its space has certainly been made the most of. The floor is carpeted with thick sheets of gray felt, and littered with chests, sacks, baskets, bark shoes, and bits of harness; while hanging from the tent poles, or thrust into the folds of the skins that cover them, are a perfect museum of things of every sort—caps, pouches, fish-spears, knives, hatchets, whips — and last, but certainly not least, the face of a baby, which has been thrust into a kind of pocket in the skin, like a knife into the sheath. I stoop to stroke the little brown face, while the round eyes stare wonderingly at me out of the folds of the skin.

Meanwhile the lady of the house (or rather tent) hospitable like all Samoiedes, hastens to set before me some black bread mixed with bark, and a lump of terrifically strong cheese, made of reindeer milk.

The reindeer supplies the Samoiedes with plenty of other things beside cheese; indeed, almost everything that they have got comes from *it* in some form or other. They eat reindeer meat, they drink reindeer milk; their fish-spears are tipped with reindeer horn; their clothes, and the very tents in which they live, are made of reindeer skin; the needles wherewith they stitch them are of reindeer bone, and the thread of reindeer sinew; and when they wish to move from place to place, it is the reindeer that draws them along — the Samoiede would be as badly off without his reindeer, as the Arab without his camel.

THE JEWELLED TOMB.

WOULD the youthful readers of this volume like to hear about the most beautiful tomb in the world?

It is in the city of Agra in India, on the other side of the globe. When Boston children are eating their lunch or playing in the sunshine at noon-recess, it is midnight in India. It is so hot there that if anyone happened to be awake, he would probably be fanning himself and looking out of the window up at the stars which are bigger and brighter than in New England, or down at the gardens where hundreds of great fireflies dart and whirl as if it were Fourth of July without the noise.

The Jewelled Tomb was built about the time when your great-great-grandfathers first came to Plymouth.

The Jewelled Tomb.

You know how cold and bleak they found it — the winds were stinging, the earth covered with ice and snow, storms were on the sea and savages on the shore. The Pilgrims made no grand tombs there; they dared not even pile up leaves to mark their graves as the robins did over the Babes in the Wood, but buried their dead in wheat-fields to be hid by the waving grain. They feared the Indians, watching to murder and scalp them, would come at night, count the graves and learn how few were left alive.

SHAH-Jehan, the Mogul Emperor, built the Jewelled Tomb. His name means King of the World, because he ruled over so many people. Jewels were like the sand of the sea to him, he owned so many. The Koh-i-noor, "the mountain of light," was his, and there is but one larger diamond in the world. The Brahmins say that the owner of the Kohi-noor will always be ruler of India.

Shah Jehan's soldiers and slaves could not be counted, and there seemed no end of his cities and palaces. One of the oldest establishments in his dominion was a hospital for sick monkeys, where kind nurses took care of the little mimics, cured or made them comfortable, while they jabbered and screeched to their hearts' content, snatched the medicine or choice fruits from their keepers, and plagued each other like wizened spoilt children. But the great Mogul did not care so much for the health of his subjects — he had so many it did not seem worth while.

He was very fond of elephant fights, and used to sit in a balcony overlooking the space between his palace and the river Jumna to watch them. Sometimes a maddened elephant had to be driven by fireworks into the river and drowned to prevent its trampling to death the whole crowd which had no balcony to see from. So many riders were killed in the sport, that one would often kiss his wife and children, saying, "Good-by, you may never see me again — I am going to amuse the Emperor — we have an elephant fight to-day." Shah-Jehan enjoyed this spectacle whether his subjects were killed or not. His balcony was hung with rich Persian silks. Diamonds and riches shone in his turban and sparkled on his breast. Every time he moved, his jewels threw rainbows over the crowd and often into the eyes of the combatants.

He had a plan of making a trellis over this balcony. The grapes were to be amethysts, the leaves emeralds, and the stalks pure gold. But one morning the head goldsmith came to him, saying: "May it please your Majesty, your trellis will take all the emeralds and amethysts in the world."

For once in his life Shah-Jehan gave up his whim and only one bunch of grapes was ever finished.

This monarch loved power and splendor, but more than all he loved his wife Moomtazee. She was the niece of the famous Noor Mahal, and was called the most beautiful woman in the world, and was good as she was beautiful. "Light of the World," "Pearl of Women," "Crown of Delight," were some of the names her husband gave her. For hours he would sit by her side in his palace garden, on seats made soft by cashmere shawls, finer than any that ever crossed the ocean. They listened to the murmur of the river; they watched the pink lilies, as large as christening cups, that floated on its waves. Great leaves and wonderful flowers, such as we see only in conservatories, bent their heads beneath the spray of the fountains. There are few singing birds in that land, but from musicians, hidden behind the trees, came melodies which mingled with the sound of rippling waters.

All this was real, and not a story from the Arabian Nights.

One evening when the glow-worms had lit their lamps under every bush, the Mogul and his Empress were in the garden. Their eldest daughter, best beloved of his children because she most resembled her mother, was playing at their feet.

"Dearest Queen," exclaimed Shah-Jehan, "here are some flowers that I have just plucked. How happy should I be if you could not die! You are lovely as these roses, and I fear some day you will fade as they do. Allah allows a little worm to destroy a shawl that it has taken a life-time to make — if some unseen enemy should take your life, there would be nothing left me but a kingdom whose sun had set."

The Queen replied: "I will never leave this earth as long as Allah will let me stay."

"Jehanara," she continued to her daughter, "if the Angel of Death should take me from your father, comfort and watch over him, and be all that your mother is to the great and good Emperor."

"Promise, my lord," she said, "if I should die, never to marry again; and place a tomb over my grave, grand as a palace, and beautiful as these flowers covered with diamond dew, that the whole world may know how the greatest of earthly monarchs loved his Moomtazee Mahal."

"I promise," said her husband, with trembling voice, "if you should leave me, no one shall ever fill your place, and the world has never seen so grand a monument as I will raise over the loveliest of women."

Soon after the Queen became ill. The Emperor was distracted when she said to him, "Remember my two requests; now I must leave you."

All the doctors and wise men in the Kingdom were summoned, but they were so afraid their heads would be cut off, they did not know what to do; they suggested so many things that of course the poor Queen stood very little chance. All the love and power of her husband could not save her any more than if she had been the wife of her meanest slave.

She died — the palace was dumb with grief. No official dared to speak to the Emperor and tell him of his loss. Jehanara put her arms softly around her father's neck and sobbed into his ear, "The Light of the World has gone out."

The funeral was scarcely over, when Shah-Jehan began to build the tomb of his wife.

In our country when we think of a monument, it is a granite shaft or a marble block; we place it in a cemetery, and plant vines and trees around it. In commemoration of many great and good men we sometimes build a high monument — like that on Bunker Hill — where we can climb to the top and look over the country, telling each other how grand the nation has become because of the patriots beneath us who gave their lives for our liberty.

But in India, diamonds are dug out of the earth, precious stones filtered from streams, and pearls fished from the seas. Every thought of nature is a jewel, and glitters in the sunshine. The beetles are living gems; the orange lizards that peep from under the stones show neck-laces of brilliants. It is the land of peacocks, whose gorgeous eyes repeat in the sunlight all the wonders under ground. No goldsmith can make such dazzling colors as the butterflies carry through the air. So when the Emperor would build a mausoleum to the Pearl of Women, he adorned it with the most splendid gems that ever shone even in that Land of Jewels.

Shah-Jehan had been collecting precious stones all his life; but though he already had a greater number than any one else in the world, he ransacked all countries for more and finer gems to adorn his work.

He brought the most skillful architects from France and Italy. The chief of them was Austin de Bordeaux, named the Jewel-handed.

Seeds planted in the garden round the edifice grew to be tall trees, and children who had watched the levelling of the great platform became middle-aged men and women before the dome - was finished. Twenty thousand workmen went home every night, year after year, always telling their families how particular the Emperor was that every stone should be placed right, till at last they grew grey-headed — for it took twenty-two years of hard work to build the tomb.

I cannot tell you how many millions it cost — there are so many different estimates given — it were as easy to tell the majorities on election night. But all agree that it cost an enormous sum.

Nothing interested Shah-Jehan but this tomb of his beautiful wife. It stood on the river Jumna in a garden two-thirds as large as Boston Common, and was surrounded by a red sand-stone wall high as the roof of most houses. The Emperor used to sit in one of the arcades on the inner side of this wall and watch the progress of the building. Careless of the terraced garden with its paths of variegated marble and its eighty fountains throwing diamonds into the air, regardless of the two mosques where Mussulmen go to pray, his eye was always fastened upon the dazzling structure which rose above all and gleamed like a mountain of snow against the blue sky.

At length the Taje Mahal, the "Crown of Edifices," was completed. Let us visit it. On the side opposite the river we pass the wall through the grand red gate-way. It seems to be ornamented with garlands, but looking closer you observe that what we mistook for flowers are texts from the Koran, the Bible of the Mahommedans. These texts are inlaid in the stone, arranged in graceful lines, and illuminated with colored marbles.

Passing through the garden, an avenue of Italian cypresses shuts us in like a pall, while a voice from the attendant comes out of the darkness, saying: "Close your eyes for a moment; you will not die, but you shall see Heaven." Emerging from between the trees, we mount to the platform which is raised eighteen feet above the highest garden terrace, and is a square of over three hundred feet, glittering and polished as ice. At each corner and separate from the main building rises a tall slender minaret, through whose open carving appears the circular stairs leading to the top. In the midst we behold the octagonal mausoleum, surmounted by four small cupolas around the central dome, which towers as high as Bunker Hill monument.

Where we stand above the world, everything beneath our feet and around us is made of white marble. There is no tinge of color on the four minarets, but within them the central pile is covered with delicate traceries that look like flowering vines. They are verses from the Koran; every letter is black marble inlaid in the white, and ornamented with jasper, agate, cornelian and lapis-lazuli. When we are told that the whole sacred book is written in this way upon the Taje Mahal, we understand why the work took twenty years.

There is an entrance north, south, east and west. Crossing the threshold of either, we see that the vast interior is divided into several apartments. Beneath each of the four small domes is a separate enclosure. Under the central dome an octagonal space is shut in by colonades roofed with arches. High above you, in the very centre of this great dome, flashes a golden ornament like a constellation of stars. The floor, the walls, the columns, the ceiling, all are of glistening white marble. About seventy-five feet from the floor a carved trellis-work around the base of the dome lights the place, and shows the whole interior to be a mosaic of texts. They are made of black letters; not straight like those in a printed book, but twisted like the tendrils of a vine; and in this central and more sacred chamber, precious stones of every color gleam and sparkle around the words as if from a thorny stem gay flowers had sprung on every side. The buds and leaves look so natural as to deceive the eye. You wonder if the whole building has been decorated for a victory; if those are garlands of evergreens and flowers that cross the arches, drip over the freizes, interlace each other and almost wave in the breeze — and if they are for a Christmas festival?

The great Mogul placed them on these walls, and they are enduring as his love.

You seem to look at banks of snow overspread with wreaths of flowers which the sun, streaming through the high trellised windows, transforms into foaming cataracts falling from the sky, while braided rainbows flash and dance on their waves.

On the floor, under the dome, is an octagonal screen, higher than a tall man, and made of marble as delicately wrought as a veil of lace. It is bordered with lilies, tulips and roses, made of precious stones. Within this screen, beneath the centre of the dome, is a slab of marble six feet in length.

The poor mother covers her darling's grave with flowers — all she can give; they fade, and she still keeps fresh tokens there. The flowers the great Mogul placed on the grave of his Queen were made of the most costly jewels. The finest rubies that he had searched the world to procure, glowed in a rose near the head, close by an emerald lotus leaf covered with diamond spray. Texts from the Koran, always in black letters, form an inlaid back ground of thorns for the flowers. Mahometans believe these texts make the grave more sacred, and are a charm to preserve it from injury. On the end of the slab next the door are conspicuous the words, " Deliver us from the tribe of unbelievers."

No royal lady's brooch was ever of more delicate workmanship than this casket of jewels. It glitters in the marble hall like a clustre of diamonds on a robe of white satin. Sparks of light dart on the screen, kindle the tracery into fire; tongues of flame speak on the floor; points of vivid light live all over the building and transfigure it into glory.

In a vault below this great hall, and just under the precious slab, Queen Moomtazee is buried. A lamp is always burning over her tomb, and a priest, whose white beard falls below his waist, chants from the Koran. A strange echo repeats his voice back and forth in the church above, till it seems to linger in the lofty dome, where an invisible choir whisper his words before they take flight to Heaven.

Shah-Jehan never married again. The tomb for his wife so occupied his thoughts that he did not know that the greatest empire in the world was slipping away from him. The Princess Jehanara kept her promise to her mother. Father and daughter daily laid fresh flowers on the jewelled slab in the Taje Mahal, and the starry roses watched the frail, living ones close their eyes and droop, while their own petals never faded.

The kingly mourner was dethroned by his crafty, cruel son, Aurengzebe, who became Emperor, and imprisoned his father in the very palace from which he used to watch the elephant fights. He had no solace in confinement but his faithful daughter. Every day he looked with infinite longing at the minarets of the mausoleum. He could see the dome which rose high above the grave of his Queen, but he could never lay a flower there. For eight years he could see the outside of his master-piece of architecture, but never again did his eyes behold the jewelled grave, which is the central thought, the heart of the Taje Mahal.

The Moguls no longer rule in the East. The Koh-i-noor, the ransom of a royal captive, belongs to Queen Victoria — the Empress of India.

The different conquerors of that country have destroyed many a marble palace, burnt many a beautiful city; but all of them, even the furious Sepoys, have left unharmed the Taje Mahal — the jewelled wonder, and it stands to-day in its perfect glory — the monument raised by the love of an Eastern despot to his beautiful wife.

A NIGHT WITH PAUL BOYTON.

"TELL me, what was the oddest experience you ever had?" said a friend of mine one day, upon the cars going West.

I had been "spinning yarns" to him, as the sailors say, for the last hundred miles of our journey, concerning a variety of queer happenings met with in the life of a journalistic Free-lance during the past ten years.

"Well, now, that's a hard question to answer," said I: "give me five minutes to think. Let's see—did I ever tell you about my cruise with Paul Boyton?"

Paul Boyton is the man, you know, with the rubber life-saving rig; has rescued lots of people from drowning; floated down most of the rivers of Europe and a good many in this country. My night's trip with him was about the strangest adventure that I could recall.

I first met Boyton at one of the towns upon the St. John's river in Florida. We were having a game of billiards together, when some whim prompted me to say:

"Mr. Boyton, I'd like to take a cruise with you sometime."

To my surprise, and perhaps not exactly to my liking, he at once assented.

"Why, that's easily done. I always have a spare suit along. We can go to-morrow, if you like."

Several of my acquaintances were within hearing, and I saw they would have a laugh at my expense if I backed down; so I responded with equal promptitude:

"All right, just count me in; but say, I don't want to leave from here. The whole town will be down at the wharf watching me floating about like a sick turtle. That would never do."

"Oh," said the jolly captain, "I'll fix that. You shall have a paddle, and when you are tired I'll tow

PAUL BOYTON.

you; besides, we will start after dark if you want to. we can go down with the tide. It will be running out at a lively rate about then."

Now I had no notion I would be taken up so suddenly by Captain Boyton; and although I did my best to look happy at the prospect, I am afraid it was a sorry effort.

A man in Texas described to me, once, his feelings after engaging to fight a duel; and I suppose that my sensations and reflections were, during the succeeding twenty-four hours, not unlike his. I lay in bed that night and thought of the watery couch that had been chosen for my next resting-place.

It was a long, very long night, full of forebodings and regrets. In the morning the clerk of the hotel kindly inquired if I wished my effects sent home by express, or detained until my friends could arrive "for the body;" the folks at the breakfast-table rallied me about it; and some of my acquaintances made bets that I would back out. When I went down the main street it seemed as though every one was pointing a finger at me, with a look that said plainly:

"That's the fellow that's going to commit suicide to-night!"

It was about half-past six in the evening when we emerged from a building close beside the water, the captain leading, and his victim, as he humorously called me, following close behind, escorted by a single lantern and a group of friends. The lantern cast a gloomy ray out upon the black surface of the river, and gave the two principal figures in their rubber disguises the aspect of some fabled amphibious monsters.

The suits were made in two parts, joined at the waist by a round iron band, over which the rubber-cloth was so well secured as to be quite water-tight. The head was covered by a hood, concealing all but the eyes, mouth, and nose. In the back of the head-piece there was an air-chamber, which, when filled, gave the voyager a very comfortable pillow. Along the sides were two more large air-chambers, and still a couple below, to support the legs.

Just as soon as we were in, or rather *upon*, the water, all sense of trepidation vanished. As the tide drifted us away from the noisy group upon the wharf

SEEING THEM OFF

and into the darkness, I was able to wave my paddle and reply to their repartee right heartily. I felt quite happy at the novelty of the thing; but wait — one of the boys shouts:

"Look out as you pass the point. I saw a big ''gator' there yesterday. Keep towards the middle!"

Alligators! I hadn't, in all my wild forebodings, taken them into consideration. A *creepy* sensation pervaded my back and travelled down to my toes. "What if — oh! I wish he hadn't shouted that," thought I.

"Well, at any rate the captain's ahead; they'll get him first, and maybe I'll have a chance while they are lunching from him!" So I turned around and remarked casually:

"I guess, Cap. you had better keep a little ahead. You know the way better than I do!"

But somehow the captain had disappeared. I shouted, and paddled rapidly in the direction I supposed him to be. No answer!

"I believe the alligators have got him already," thought I; and you should have seen the way that paddle went through the water, driving me back toward the distant wharf where the lantern still twinkled. My foot encountered something.

Oh, *horrors!* what a yell I gave! You can wager that brief second will never be forgotten. No, sir! But it was only a stray log; and just then the captain's merry laugh resounded over the water close at hand, as he came floating toward me, delighted with the success of his trick; and he began to sing a song of his own composing, improvising the music and splashing his paddle in time to his melody:

> "I'll take my sleep on the rolling deep,
> Your downy couch let others keep;
> My paddle true will guide me through,
> My life-garb is better than any canoe;—
> Whoop! hurrah! yes, than any canoe!"

The echoes of the refrain died away among the woods of the far opposite shore, startling a brood of wild fowl from their rest in the sedge of the bayou.

Now the captain turned and said, "Let's give 'em a rocket!"

I have forgotten to tell you that the captain had in

"LET'S GIVE THEM A ROCKET."

tow a miniature craft, which he fondly called *Baby Mine*. It was made of tin, and was altogether a miraculous sort of boat, as I soon discovered, for it held all sorts of things one might want for comfort upon or *in* the water.

Baby Mine was entirely decked in, having a tin "hatch," into which the captain put his hand and produced a small lamp, which was fitted to a groove in the bows. This was lighted by means of matches, and a rocket next appeared. The latter was fixed in an upright position upon *Baby Mine*. The captain held the boat with one hand and touched off the rocket with the other.

Whiz-z-z-z-z!

And away it sped into the black sky above, and then:

Bang!

A myriad of tiny sparkles flew outward and then fell slowly, streaking the sky for a moment with a rainbow of fire. We could see in the pallid light the group that still lingered upon the wharf, half a mile away.

"Now," said Boyton, "let's have a little stage effect."

So he took from the interior of *Baby Mine* a tin saucer and a wooden float, as well as some powder in a small bottle. He poured a little of the latter upon the dish and set it upon the float. A match was applied to a short fuse. As soon as ignited, the powder cast a brilliant lurid glow over the wavelets, and we seemed to be floating in a literal sea of blood. In the midst of this — shall I ever forget that ludicrous sight? — was the captain, grimacing out of his hood like some horrid satyr, and wagging his two black paws like a great pair of ears. I can't do the subject justice. Perhaps you may have dreamed of some such personage after taking a late and too hearty supper.

All of this time the captain had been standing upright in the water, head and shoulders out, looking as firm as though he was upon the bottom, although I knew the river must be at least forty feet deep where we were.

"Now you must learn how to stand," said he; and after a few failures I was able to take an upright position or lie down at will.

The tide had soon carried us beyond the point and

its fabled alligators, at which the captain laughed with contempt.

"Look at this knife," cried he. "I've killed *sharks* with this, and wouldn't be afraid to try it on an alligator." He produced a long, peculiar Turkish blade from his belt, and made a lunge at an imaginary saurian.

The moon had now cleared the low-hanging mists of the night, and we could see our course fairly well. Ahead of us we noticed a second point, and oh, listen! out of its reeds there came the sound of some heavy body, and something black moved from the shore. It made an ominous splashing as it came towards us. Even the brave captain, forgetful of his knife and boast, eyed it dubiously. I shook all over; the water seemed to have suddenly become as cold as ice. Just then the captain's cheerful laugh came like music to my ears.

"That isn't an alligator;" he whispered, "it's a darkey in a dug-out. Keep quiet, and we'll have some fun."

The captain quickly and silently produced his pan and red fire. We floated like logs on the water until the boatman had almost reached us, and then a sudden and unaccountable blaze sprang out of the waters before his horrified gaze, while two undoubted demons emerged and waved their arms towards him with horrid groans.

It was enough — far more than enough. With a screech of terror the black man sprang from his boat and struck out for shore, uttering dismal entreaties to "good Mister Debbil" not to "ketch him yet," with every plunge; and despite our calls, he broke through the reeds, clambered up the bank, and was soon lost to hearing in the dense forest.

Sometimes, when I think of it, I wonder if that chap is running yet; but I guess he brought up somewhere, for we heard soon afterwards that there was a great gathering of the negroes, and that one of their speakers had seen a couple of monsters rising out of the waters of the St. John's, commanding him to tell the people the world was coming to an end.

"Now that was rather lively, hey?" mused the captain; "but I'm sorry we scared him so. I wonder what's in his boat? We're pirates now, to all intents

SUDDEN AND UNACCOUNTABLE.

and purposes, and may as well take our plunder. A bag of potatoes — no, oranges, just what I wanted. No wonder he ran so — he's been into one of the groves over there. I wonder if it's stealing to steal from a thief? Let's have some supper. I nearly forgot about supper."

A loose plank was taken from the dug-out, and out of the wonderful depths of *Baby Mine* emerged the following items:

A quart bottle of cold coffee,

A can of condensed milk,

Some loaf-sugar,

A tin box of cheese,

Four biscuits,

A pot of marmalade,

Some chipped beef,

A half-dozen boiled eggs,

Pickles, pepper and salt,

Spoons,

Knives,

Tin cups,

Etc.

"The company will please sit down, and excuse

the holes in the cloth, and not put their elbows on the table," said the jolly captain, as he held the coffee over the lamp while I 'set' the table.

"Now, here we go! What an appetite I've got! Don't lean back in your chair, my boy, one of the legs is gone; you might upset. I wish that chap had stayed. He might have taken tea with us, at least. Halloo! I've struck bottom. We're right in shore. I guess the tide's about ebb!" and so the merry fellow rattled on, taking a look at his watch, which hung upon some peg in the cabin of *Baby Mine*.

What a surpassingly beautiful place we had drifted into! A cove, surrounded upon three sides by great water oaks that bent their long arms down towards the tide, draped in sad but rich festoons of gray Spanish moss. The pale forms of dead cypress trees, swathed in wild grape-vines, leaned over, and fragrant magnolia branches mingled their dark and glossy leaves through all the fairy tracery of branch and palm, displayed like dark embroidery against the moonlit heavens. How I wished the boys could be there to see us now!

It was altogether the queerest supper I ever swal-

TAKING TEA WITH CAPTAIN BOYTON.

lowed. From the still well-stored depths of the tin boat the captain produced a cigar-case, and presently we reclined at ease upon our aqueous couch, waiting for the tide to run in again. What tales the captain told that night, as we lay there! what recitals of his adventures in other lands; of receptions by monarchs; of his famous voyage down the terrible and mysterious Tagus; of the queer people he met in the Spanish provinces; of his feats in Russia — why! I could fill a book with them.

About two o'clock we found ourselves drifting out into the river again, and were soon making good headway towards home. For an hour we paddled side by side, but my unaccustomed arms began to fail, and then the captain unwound a blue-fish line from a reel and tied it to my foot, so he towed me along; and released from the need of action, I lay upon my snug air-pillow and watched the waning moon.

Just as the early tints began to paint the eastern sky, foretelling the coming of sunrise (will you believe me?), I actually fell asleep.

When I aroused myself it was quite light and we

were passing the last point; and there, upon a log, lay stretched out my friend's alligator, gazing sleepily at us, but never deigning to move.

I wonder if he realized what a dainty meal he might have had!

BOY-DIVERS IN THE RED SEA.

"HERE we are at last, Mr. Ker," says the captain, as we cast anchor off the coast of Arabia, a little after sunset, about two-thirds down the Red Sea. "It's too dark to make out much to-night, but you'll see a rare sight when you come on deck to-morrow morning."

The worthy captain's mention of "coming on deck" is doubtless from force of habit, for neither he nor I have been anywhere *but* on deck for more than a week, except perhaps to look for something which we have left below. Most of my time is spent in the rigging, where what little wind there is may generally be met with; and our table-cloth is spread on the "after-hatch," while our arrangements for going to bed consist merely of throwing a blanket on the deck, and stretching ourselves upon it, undisturbed save by an occasional scamper of two or three frolicsome rats over our faces.

When I awake the next morning, I find the captain's promise amply made good. The sun is just rising, and under its golden splendor the broad blue sea stretches westward as far as eye can reach, every ripple tipped with living fire. On the other side extends a sea of another kind — the gray, unending level of the great Arabian desert, melting dimly into the warm dreamy sky. In front, the low white wall of a Turkish fort stands out like an ivory carving against the hot brassy yellow of the sand-hills that line the shore; while all around it are the little cabins of mud-plastered wickerwork that compose the Arab village, looking very much like hampers left behind by some monster picnic. Here and there, through the light green of the shallower water along the shore, a flash of dazzling white, keen and narrow as the edge of a sword, marks the presence of the dangerous coral-reefs among which we have been picking our way for the last three days, with the chance of running aground at any moment.

"You were right, captain," say I, as the burly skipper rises and stretches his brawny arms, like a bear awaking from its winter nap. "This is a sight worth seeing, indeed."

"Ah, *this* ain't what I meant," chuckles the captain; "the best o' the show's to come yet. Look over yonder — there, just 'twixt the reef and the shore. D'ye see anything in the water?"

"Well, I think I see something swimming — sharks, I suppose."

"Sharks, eh? Well, *land*-sharks you might call 'em, p'raps. Take my glass and try again."

The first look through the glass works a startling change. In a moment the swarm of round black spots which I have ignorantly taken for the backs of sharks, are turned into *faces* — the faces of Arab children, and (as I perceive with no little amazement) of very young children too, some of the smallest being apparently not more than five or six years old! Our vessel is certainly not less than a mile from the shore, and the water, shallow as it is, is deep enough at any point to drown the very tallest of these adventurous little "water-babies;" yet they are evidently making for the ship, and that, too, at a speed that will soon bring them alongside of her.

"Are they really coming all this way out without resting?" ask I.

"Bless you, that's nothing to an Arab!" laughs the captain; "these little darkies are as much at home in the water as on land. I've heard folks talk a good deal of the way the South Sea Islanders can swim; but I've seen as good swimming here as ever I saw there."

And now, as the Lilliputian swimmers draw nearer, we begin to hear their shrill cries and elfish laughter; and now they are close enough for their little brown faces, and glittering teeth, and beady black eyes, to be easily distinguished; and now one final stroke of their lean sinewy arms carries them alongside, and the blue water swarms with tiny figures, looking up and waving their hands so eagerly that one might almost expect to hear them call out, "Shine, boss?" and see them produce a brush and a pot of blacking. But instead of that, there is a universal chorus of "*Piastre, Howadji!*" (a penny, my lord!)

"Chuck 'em a copper, and you'll see something good!" says the captain,

I rummage the few remaining pockets of my tattered white jacket, and at last unearth a Turkish piastre (5 cts.) which I toss into the water. Instantly the smooth bright surface is dappled with a forest of tiny brown toes, all turning upward at once, and down plunge the boy-divers, their supple limbs glancing through the clear water like a shoal of fish.

By this time nearly all the crew are looking over the side, and encouraging the swimmers with lusty shouts; for, used as Jack is to all sorts of queer spectacles, this is one of which he seems never to tire.

"There's one of 'em got it!"

"No, he ain't!"

"Yes, he has — I see him a-comin' up with it!"

"And there's the others a-tryin' to take it from him — hold tight, Sambo!"

Sure enough, the successful diver is surrounded by three or four piratical comrades, who are doing their best to snatch away the hard-won coin; but he sticks to it like a man, and as he reaches the surface, holds it up to us triumphantly, and then pops it into his mouth — the only pocket he has got.

But this is a sad mistake on his part. In a moment a crafty companion swims up behind him, and tickles him under the chin. As his mouth opens, out drops the coin into his assailant's hand, from whom it is instantly snatched by some one else; and a regular bear-fight ensues in the water, which splashes up all around them like a fountain-jet, while their shouts and laughter make the air ring.

"Aren't they afraid of sharks?" ask I of the captain, who has just increased the confusion tenfold by throwing another copper into the very midst of the screaming throng.

"Not they — they make too much row for any shark to come near *them*. Sharks are mighty easy scared, for all they're so savage. You'll never catch 'em coming too near a steamer when she's goin' — the flappin' of the screw frightens 'em away. See, there's two of 'em comin' along now, and you'll just see how much the boys'll care for 'em."

And, indeed, the sudden uprising of those gaunt black fins, piercing the smooth water as with an unexpected stab, seems to produce no effect whatever upon these fearless urchins, who paddle about as unconcerned as ever. Moreover, it soon appears that the sharks themselves have other business to attend to. A shoal of flying-fish come driving past, glistening like rainbows in the dazzling sunshine as they leap out of the water and fall back again. Instantly one of the "sea-lawyers" dashes at the rear of the column, while the other, wheeling around its front, heads back the fugitives into his comrade's open jaws; and in this way the two partners contrive to make a very respectable "haul."

But at this moment the garrison-boat is seen putting off from the shore, with one of the Pasha's officers in the stern-sheets. At sight of the well-known official flag, our water-babies scatter like wild-fowl, and the next moment all the little black heads are seen bobbing over the shining ripples on their way back to the shore.

ST. BOTOLPH'S TOWN.

LONG time ago, there were in England, as well as in many other countries, certain pious men and women who, for their eminent wisdom, charitable works, or lives of purity and usefulness, came to be called Saints.

Among these was a Saxon monk, the Abbot of Ikanho, St. Botolph by name, who lived about the middle of the seventh century.

Botolph belonged to a noble English family. After having been educated at one of the religious houses in what was then called Belgic Gaul, he came back to England, and begged of King Ethelmund a barren spot on which to build a monastery; and here, on the Witham River, near the eastern coast of England, in what is now called Lincolnshire, he built his priory, and founded a town to which was given the name, St. Botolph's Town.

Here is what an unknown poet says of it in Longfellow's *Poems of Places:*

> "St. Botolph's Town! — Hither across the plains
> And fens of Lincolnshire, in garb austere,
> There came a Saxon monk, and founded here
> A priory, pillaged by marauding Danes,
> So that thereof no vestige now remains;
> Only a name, that spoken loud and clear,
> And echoed in another hemisphere,
> Survives the sculptured walls and painted panes.
> St. Botolph's Town! — Far over leagues of land
> And leagues of sea looks forth its noble tower,
> And far around the chiming bells are heard."

Now as the English people have a queer way of shortening names, as the years go on, that reminds one of the riddle:

> "Little Nan Etticoat has a white petticoat
>   And a red nose.
> The longer she stands the shorter she grows."

In process of time old St. Botolph's Town became reduced to simply *Boston.**

So now you see that that "echo in another hemisphere" of St. Botolph's Town is, of course, the name of our own Boston, so called by its early English set-

---
*St. Botolph's Bridge in Huntingdonshire is now called Bottle-Bride!

tlers in memory of the English Boston they had left behind them; though, as those of you who have read Higginson's History know, it had at first borne the name of Trimountain, because of its three hills; its Indian name having been Mushauwomuck, shortened, English fashion, to Shawmut. Boston school-boys, never forget that the original Indian name meant Free-country, or Free-land!

The name Botolph means "*Boat-help;*" and so, in those old times St. Botolph came to be deemed the patron saint of mariners; and as both Bostons are commercial cities by the sea, it is eminently appropriate that they should bear the old Boat-helper's name. Perhaps, too, that is why "Simon Kempthorn, Mariner," in Longfellow's *New England Tragedy* of *John Endicott*, cries out, when a fire is kindled in Boston's Market Place, in the year 1656, to burn the religious books of the persecuted Quakers:

" Rain, rain, rain,
Bones of St. Botolph, and put out this fire!"

(Would not that quotation make a capital motto for a Boston Fire Company!)

The English Boston has a high church-tower, one of the most beautiful in England,

> "The loftiest tower of Britain's isle,
> In valley or on steep."

It resembles the tower of Antwerp Cathedral, and is crowned by a beautiful octagonal lantern, that can be seen forty miles off. It serves, therefore, as a landmark for seamen.

Another poet in *Poems of Places* says:

> "Beneath that lordly tower
> A simple chapel stands,
> In days long gone it caught the sound
> Of Cotton's earnest tongue."

For the Reverend John Cotton, one of Boston's earliest ministers, came from Boston, England; and it is of him that "Norton" says, in the *Tragedy of John Endicott:*

> "'The lantern of St. Botolph's ceased to burn
> When from the portals of that church he came
> To be a burning and a shining light
> Here in the wilderness."

And now I have to tell you of what seems to me a pleasing and surprising coincidence:

In the Catholic calendar each saint has his special day; thus, you know we have St. Valentine's Day, on Feb. 14th, when you send the pretty valentines; St. Patrick's Day, March 17th, when our Irish citizens march in processions, "wearing of the green;" St. John's Day, June 24th, when the Canadians among us make wreaths and garlands of the fresh young maple-leaves, because the maple is the Canadian emblem. Now it so happens that St. Botolph's Day is, of all days in the year for the American Boston's patron saint — what do you think? *The Seventeenth of June!*

That Seventeenth of June, when Boston puts on her very best gala dress, when the bells all ring, and the Fire Companies form into processions, and the Military march, and the orators make speeches, and the children sing, and the great organ makes grand patriotic music, and the stars and stripes are flung to the "Boston east-winds," and the holiday is a jolly day!

Now do not you agree with me that we have found

a delightful triple coincidence, in that Boston's great holiday is Bunker Hill Day; and Bunker Hill Day is the Seventeenth of June; and the Seventeenth of June is old St. Botolph's Day?

SOME QUEER AMERICANS.

THE queerest people in this country, I fancy, live down in the southern part of the Blue Ridge where that magnificent range of mountains passes through the northern parts of both Carolinas and of Georgia. Even their houses are small and queer, and all their tools and machinery of the most primitive description.

The farm-houses through the mountains are made of logs, and, as the weather is not usually very cold, the chinking of mud and chips between the logs is very likely to fall out and be only half replaced, so that in the storms of winter, they must be comfortless abodes; but, as I said, the cold comes mainly in the shape of sudden storms after which there is a warm spell. You remember, that when the stranger asked Kit, the famous " Arkansas Traveller," why he didn't patch the hole in his roof, he answered "that it had been so all-fired rainy he couldn't."

"But why don't you now that it doesn't rain?"

"Because now it don't leak!" cried Kit triumphantly, and went on with his fiddling.

Well, that is a very good example of the spirit which builds these houses and tries to keep them — not in repair exactly, but at least upright. I am speaking of the ordinary farm-houses in the mountains. Now and then you will see more snug and pretentious ones, but not often even among men who own several hundred acres of land and a large number of cows, horses and sheep. Sometimes they build two log huts pretty close together, and roof over the space between, making an open hall-way or store-shed, where saddles, and dried fruit are hung, and where all sorts of things are placed out of the rain or sun. In nearly every case, too, the roof of the front side of the house is continued out into a broad shed, where benches are placed, and half the household work is done I have often seen the loom upon which they wove their homespun clothes filling up half the space in this broad porch, and shaded by masses of morning glory, Virginia creeper or columbine. A low log house with one of these long-roofed porches reminds one of a man with a slouched hat pulled down over his eyes.

Whether the house is large or small; such as I have described or better than that; you will be sure to see the chimney wholly on the outside. It stands at the end of the house, and is a huge pile of stone set in mortar or perhaps only a conglomerate of sticks and stones and mud, half as wide as the house itself at the base, and then narrowing somewhat to the summit six or eight feet above the gable. The great summer house of Mr. John C. Calhoun, the famous senator who died about twenty years ago, has two of these big outside chimneys made of brick; and this mansion was considered a very grand one in its day.

If you should go inside — and the women and children are very hospitable to strangers — you would find little evidence of what we in the north call comfort. There will be one large room, serving as sitting-room, dining-room and kitchen, nearly one whole side of which will be given up to the vast fireplace

"SWEET HOME" IN THE MOUNTAINS.

which is hollowed into the broad chimney. On the opposite side from the fire, perhaps, will be a little bedroom partitioned off, but often not, and the only other room in the house will be the rough boarded attic overhead, reached by a ladder. Lathing and plastering are hardly known outside the few villages, and carpets are still more rare. A bedstead or two, some splint-bottomed home-made chairs, as straight-backed and uncomfortable as possible, a rough table and some benches complete the furniture. Stoves are not yet known to the mountaineers. They cling to the old-fashioned way of cooking at the open fire-place, hanging the iron pot in which they boil their food over the fire upon a swinging iron arm fixed in the side of the chimney and called a "crane;" or if they want to roast a spare-rib of beef or pork, hanging that by a hook upon the crane, and steadily turning it round until it is evenly done.

Another favorite dish is the hoe-cake or corn-dodger, which is a batter-cake of corn-meal baked before the open fire, or in the bottom of the iron pot. Wheat flour is almost unknown in some of these mountain districts, cornmeal and sorghum molasses wholly taking its place. The mills where it is ground are the most picturesque and seemingly useless affairs. Every mile or so through these rough hills there comes tumbling down a clear and rapid stream, so that water-power is plenty enough for each man to have his own mill, and most of them are essentially home-made. I saw one over near the sources of the Chestatee which from the outside looked far more like a heap of old drifted logs than anything else. The man who ran it built the whole affair himself, with only an axe, a saw and a two-inch auger for tools. The entire running-gear was wooden, yet this mill had stood many years and ground all the corn of the neighborhood. Such machinery is slow and weak of course, but the people who use it have plenty of time. They can't understand the hurry and anxiety to save time which characterize their more thrifty neighbors who live *in* the world instead of alongside of it.

A boy who was not born in the mountains, and was used to livelier motions, took some corn to one of these Georgia mills to be ground not long ago, succeeded in waking the miller up, getting the wheel in

AN INTERIOR.

motion and his grist in the hopper. Then, expecting a long delay, he wandered off. But when he came back his meal was not half ready and he became impatient.

"My chickens — and thar ain't but two of 'em either — would eat meal faster'n yer mill'll grind it!"

"How long could they keep it up?" asked the miller.

"Until they starved to death," replied the smart boy.

This is the only boy, however, whom I ever heard complain of the slowness of life there, for none of them are accustomed to anything faster, except when they are on horseback. Then the young chaps make the road fly from under them, and ride their fine horses with great spirit. On horseback is the usual method of travel, indeed, for the roads over the mountains are exceedingly rough, and to many farms there is hardly any road at all for wheels.

One day we were riding gayly along on a couple of the excellent saddle-horses that are so common among these hills, when we came to the banks of the Etowah river. There was no bridge, and the road led right down to the low banks, and through the amber-clear water we could see the tracks of the wagons which had crossed before us. I had heard of the Etowah many times as one of the most beautiful rivers of Georgia, and I am glad to pass the reputation along. I remembered, also, that in place of the beads of wood, soapstone and various sorts of shell which are dug up as the remains of some Indian girl's necklace, or red man's earring, on the banks of this river beads of pure gold had been found. The Indians here were rich — they had golden ornaments instead of shell-wampum; but their gold proved their ruin, for the poor Cherokees were driven away as soon as their wealth was discovered and white men hastened to wash the sands of this troubled river. But I did not set out to describe the gold mines, but only to show why the Etowah particularly interested me, and why I was glad to find it equal to its praise.

However, I was not given much time for quiet delight. On the bank, by the side of the road, sat two lank and rough-looking Georgians with scowls on their faces. As we trotted near they rose up and came to meet us, while one sung out:

GRIST-MILL ON THE CHESTATEE.

"Say, mister, can't yer set weuns acrost tha'? Weem ben waitin' hyar I reckon about two hours, and them lazy fellars"—pointing over to where half a dozen men lay stretched out in the sun, smoking, with a small boat drawn up on the beach—"wouldn't pay no 'tention to our yellin'. Just let go o' your stirrup will you?"

Evidently he did not propose to lose this chance, for before I could move my foot he had pulled away the stirrup, seized the cantle of the saddle and swung himself behind me, astride my surprised horse. The other man did the same thing by my friend, and there we were, captured by the long arms that reached easily all round our waists, and had several inches to spare.

"Get up," my passenger shouted, digging his heels into my nag's flanks in a way that started him into the water with a very sudden splash, and on we went. The river was pretty deep in the middle, but we picked up our feet and got safely across to where the smokers grinned at the trouble their lazy discourtesy had forced upon us, as at a good joke. Then my man skipped off to the ground, and sliding his hand into a ragged pocket, asked with a whine:

"What do you charge?"

I doubt if he had a penny about him, for he seemed greatly relieved when I very quickly assured him he was welcome to his ferriage.

"Do you know who those fellows were?" asked my companion, as we cantered up the gravelly hill; "my man told me that they were both preachers."

"Preachers!" I said. "I took them for moonshiners at the very least."

But now and then a vehicle so strange as to bring a laugh upon the faces of even the neighbors will come down from the backwoods. The cart will have only two large heavy wheels, and these alone of all its parts will be shop-made. The massive axle-tree, and pole or shafts and the rough box were made at home — perhaps wholly chopped out with an axe and fastened together with wooden pins. You must not expect to see a horse or a span of horses drawing this odd, unpainted cart — if the owner has horses, he probably considers them worthy of the saddle only — but oxen, or an ox and cow, or only one of either sex; I heard, indeed, of one case where a cow and a donkey were hitched up together, but that was

A LIFT OVER THE FORD.

certainly extraordinary. A single cow in the traces makes the funniest picture, I think. The harness will be partly leather, partly rope, perhaps eked out with twisted bark, and from the horns a single thin rope goes back to the driver, who can thus keep his

A MOUNTAIN CONVEYANCE.

beast awake by frequent jerks. Sometimes when the mountaineer and his wife go to market they place a couple of splint chairs in the cart to sit on, like a small edition of the celebrated Florida "gondola," but as a rule there is no seat — to make one permanently would be altogether too much trouble,— and the man and his family all huddle together in the bottom of the jolting box.

Until lately these mountain people made nearly all the clothes they wore. They had hand-looms which they built themselves, and it was the occupation of the women at all spare moments to spin the flax or the wool, to dye the yarn and weave the cloth. These looms are just the same rough picturesque old machines that used to be seen all over the country before the Revolution, but which now exist only in some out of the way corners, like this Blue Ridge region. Before the year's weaving begins the whole house presents a gay appearance, for from every peg and place where they can be hung depend brightly colored hanks of yarn ready for the loom.

The ordinary dress of the men now is this tough homespun dyed butternut color; nearly all the bed-linen and under-clothing, also, of the mountain people, is still made by them. But the women's calico dresses are bought at the village store and made after very wonderful patterns. The only head dress is the universal Shaker sun-bonnet. On Sundays, however, if some travelling preacher happens along and holds service in the tumble down meeting-house at the four corners, you will see black store clothes of ancient make, while the gayest of ribbons and flaunting feathers bedeck the red-cheeked and happy-hearted lassies. But this happens only once in four weeks or so, for the neighborhoods are too thinly settled and poor to support a steady minister.

Though so far behind the times in all that seems civilized and comfortable, though so ignorant of what is going on in the great world outside of their blue, beautiful mountains, and so utterly unlearned, these mountain people are warm-hearted, generous, independent in thought and faithful to a friend. They know that they are strong of frame, and have a profound contempt for those

A MOUNTAIN LASS.

who live outside in the lowlands, even for those who

live anywhere in towns, of the ways of which they know and care nothing at all. What is a man good for, they wonder, who can't ride a wild colt, or follow easily the trail of a wolf, or even track a bee to its tree? Even the women regard the men of the lower country as effeminate. A hunting party from South Carolina were up at Mt. Johah one day, when they found themselves being greatly laughed at by a young woman there, who proposed to take the largest of them on her shoulders and then run a foot-race; she said she could beat them all, thus weighted. On another occasion this same girl was seen coming out of a gorge with a rifle in her hand, her sleeves rolled up and her arms covered with blood. Upon being questioned she carelessly replied that she'd "killed a bar jest beyant the Terapin!"

Their ignorance of town ways has been the source of much amusement to city people when occasionally some of the mountain folks stray down to Atlanta or Greenville. There never were any rustics so rural, I believe. It is laughable merely to look at them. What would excite our respect for its strength and honesty on some wild hill-top, only makes them doubly ridiculous in the city's strange streets. A good story has come down from the old days before railroads, on this point.

A large party of "Hard-shell Baptists" from the Blue Ridge went down to Augusta, in wagons, one August, to buy supplies. While there, one of the brethren lost his head through drinking a glass of brandy which had been mixed with ice and sugar until it was very delicious. On his return home he was dealt with by the church. He freely acknowledged the fault, but said that he had been deceived by the "sweetnin'." The church council thereupon forgave him easily the wrong of being drunk, but expelled him for the lie he told about having *ice* in his tumbler, in midsummer, when everybody knew it was colder upon the mountains than down at Augusta, yet there was no ice!

But little by little this old, charmingly ignorant and simple mountain people, are being modernized by the running of railways past, if not through, their mountains, and the increased number of visitors that go to see their bold crags and lovely valleys. The old men and women still cling to their old ways. "'Pars like 'twould take a power to change me," one dear old lady said to me. But the boys and girls are getting more "peart," are anxious to learn and see, and are not afraid of a little change. When the Piedmont Air Line proposed to put a branch back into the hills toward the gold diggings around Dahlonega, I heard a mountain family discussing it. The daughter and pride of the household, a gushing damsel of seventeen, put in her opinion:

"Uncle Jim saays if he was to see one of them railroads a cummin' he'd leave the world and take a saplin'. Dad saays he'd just lie right down flat on the yearth. But I want 'em to come. I'd just set right down on a basket of cohn turned ovah, and clap my hands. I ain't afraid."

Then she caught me making a note, as she thought, and instantly begged me to stop.

"Some of these yere folks are right foolish," she said, half ashamed, "and maybe you'll make a heap of fun outen 'em; but you must brush 'em up a powerful lot. You musn't give 'em too much of their nat'l appearance."

Well, I hope I haven't!

THE BOY KING OF EGYPT.

YOU have all heard of Rameses the Great, whose noble presence looms up from the black night of ages, majestic, gracious, clear cut, and real almost as the monarchs of to-day.

Rameses mei Amoun, as his people delighted to call him, meaning Rameses beloved of Ammon, the great god of Egypt, was born more than three thousand years ago, in Thebes, the capital of the kingdom. His father was a pharaoh, Seti I., and his mother was the queen Livea. Old Greek historians tell marvellous stories concerning his birth. They claim that one of the gods announced to Seti in a dream that the tiny babe should become the sovereign of the whole earth. It is clear that the ambition of the father prompted him to do all in his power to secure the fulfilment of this prophecy.

With a royal liberality, he ordered that all of the male children of the realm born on the same day with the crown prince should be brought to the palace. Here nurses were provided, and they were reared with and educated like the young prince in all respects. The king believed that a company of fellow students and playmates from childhood would be bound to him in manhood by the ties of affection, the best and strongest of all. They were "skilled in all the learning of the Egyptians," and also trained to feats of bodily skill, strength and endurance. Thus they grew up a brave company of hardy young warriors, well fitted to obey and to command.

The stone pictures of Rameses on the monuments show that he was regarded as a king even in infancy, and received the homage of the people in his cradle. There are sculptures of him as a mere infant, with the finger to the mouth, and yet wearing the "pshent," or double crown of Upper and Lower Egypt. Others are in child's dress and with the braided sidelock of hair, but having the Urœus, or Asp, the symbol of royalty, above his head. These may be seen at the museum of the Louvre in Paris.

The inscriptions give us an address of his subjects to him after he had succeeded to the throne: "When you were yet a very little child, wearing the braided hair, no monument was made without you. You commanded armies when you were ten years old."

Seti, his father, died when he was but fifteen years old, and after the customary seventy days of mourning for the king had passed and his splendid tomb was sacredly sealed, Rameses II. became the boy king of the mighty land of the Nile.

The first public acts of his reign show a knowledge of human nature beyond his years. He appointed his young companions the generals of his armies; he distributed among them lands and large gifts, and by every means sought to strengthen the bands of their loyalty to himself. For the people at large he forgave all fines and penalties, and opened the doors of all the crowded prisons. In this way he secured the loving faithfulness of his subjects at home, and of the great armies he was to lead in long victorious marches through an enemy's country. Does it not read like a romance, that some of his boldest expeditions and bravest conquests were accomplished while he was still under twenty years of age? Is he not a veritable boy king? Herodotus tells us that after Ethiopia and all the nations of Asia were subdued, he passed into Europe and conquered a few wild tribes of barbarians. After each victory he erected *stelæ*, or tablets, inscribed with his name and that of his country. Herodotus saw three of these tablets, and they have been found by travellers in our day. Two of them are in Palestine. Each is the figure colossal of a warrior, carved on a solid wall of rock, standing with spear in one hand and bow in the other. On the breast is the inscription, "It is I who have conquered this country by the strength of my arm." All of his victories are also recorded on the stone walls of temples, with marvellous detail. The painted sculpture shows the wealth of tribute he exacted: gold, ivory, ebony, and timber for building his ships of war, the droves of dusky captives running before his royal chariot, and the gods bestowing honors and blessing on their well-beloved son. No monarch of earth has left a more imperishable record on the pages of history than Rameses the Great. He was the Sesostris of the Greeks, their greatest hero. He was the pharaoh whose reign was the golden age of power and splendor in Egypt. He was one of the long line who so cruelly oppressed the Israelites. Many of the magnificent monuments of his reign were builded entirely by subjugated peoples who were prisoners of war. This fact is carefully noted on tablets, and among them the "bricks without straw" of the captive Hebrews are largely represented. He is said to be the father of the princess who found the Jewish infant in his frail cradle of reeds. If this be true it was at his imperial court that Moses became "skilled in all the learning of the Egyptians." The splendid achievements of his reign attest their wonderful knowledge of the arts and sciences.

On a *stele*, or tablet, deciphered jointly by distinguished English and French orientalists, is a detailed account of the boring of an artesian well by the special decree of Rameses. An embassage, consisting of the chief dignitaries of a distant province, arrived at the court and begged an audience with the king. They petitioned for a spring to supply water to the slaves and animals employed in bringing gold from a far region over a parched desert road, and who they said were dying of thirst on the long journey. His majesty graciously had compassion on these his humble subjects, and in obedience to his royal mandate, water rose to the height of twenty feet on the road to Okan. The exact height was decreed by his own lips, and the dry and thirsty land was refreshed. The great canal from the Nile to the Red Sea — one of the triumphant successes of our own century — was first accomplished by the engineers of Rameses mei Amoun. The great temple palaces of Luxor and Karnak, the wonderful rock-hewn temples at Aboo Simbel and the Rameseum — or Memnonium, as it has been wrongly called — are among the stupendous monuments of his reign, the latter being his splendid tomb. Its walls are covered with painted sculptures telling the wonders of his life. Chief among these is an episode in one of his battles with the Khetas, a powerful enemy, which commemorates the great personal bravery of the king. It is a favorite subject of the sculptures of his time. It is twice given in the Rameseum and appears again three times in the principal temples that perpetuate the glories of his long reign of sixty-eight years.

He is represented in his chariot, furiously driven by his master of the horse into the midst of the foe, and although surrounded by the archers of the hostile ranks, he is dealing death with each arrow that flies from his strong bow, while he seems to bear a charmed life. The picture story of this dashing, reckless courage is curiously confirmed by a papyrus or Egyptian book in the British museum. This is an historical poem commemorating the battle, and written at the time by a court poet named Penta-ur. It was held in high honor by his countrymen, and was deemed worthy of a place on one of the walls of the temple palace of Karnak, where it is graven entire. It says," Six times the king pierced his way into the army of the vile Khetas, six times did he enter their midst . . . When my master of horse saw that I remained surrounded by many chariots he faltered and his heart gave way for fear; a mighty terror seized his limbs, and he cried, 'My good master, generous king, halt in thy course and let us save the breath of our lives. What can we do, O Rameses mei Amoun, my good master?' And thus did his majesty reply: ' Have courage! strengthen thy heart, oh my comrade! . . . Ammon would not be a god did he not make glorious my countenance in the presence of the countless legions of the foe.'"

The portrait statues of Rameses are innumerable, from the delicately carved statuette to the huge fragments of the Colossus of the Rameseum, which was thirteen yards in height. It would seem that his majestic figure and gracious face can never be forgotten by the race of men.

There are sphinxes of rose-colored granite with the body of a lion and the noble head of Rameses. This combination, so familiar in Egypt, typified the union of physical and intellectual strength by the lion and the man. The far-famed sitting statues in front of the "Speos," or excavated rock temple at Aboo Simbel, are the most tremendous of these portraits. Nothing even in Egypt compares with these stone giants for grandeur and power. Their measureless, voiceless, eternal strength oppresses the beholder with a sense of utter insignificance in their mighty presence. In the great halls which pierce the solid mass of the mountain, gigantic standing figures, with folded arms and the calm, placid face of Rameses, seem to uphold the everlasting hills. In another temple he is found seated between two of the gods of the land as their equal in the triad. In the rock temples of Aboo Simbel we find one of those strangely beautiful " touches of nature ' that " make the world akin." By the side of the greater one, guarded by its gigantic wardens, there is another and smaller one, called the " Speos of Athor," the goddess of love and beauty, and the " Grotto of Purity." It was built by Rameses for the sole use of his royal wife, called "Nofre-ari," "the good companion." The other temples of the country preserve the records of many kings. The one at Aboo Simbel is sacred to the glory and greatness of Rameses mei Amoun. It is by this one, then, that he builded the chapel for his queen On the wonderful front wall of the Portico are portrait statues of the royal lady and her children, and over them the legend, " Rameses, to the royal spouse, Nofre-ari, whom *he loved.*" The adamantine stone has safely brought down to us the tender grace of this dedication.

Travellers tell us that every detail of ornament in the grottoes, the pillars and their flower-like capitals, the sculpture and frescoes, are all in some way connected with the beloved wife. As a token of her grateful recognition of this knightly devotion, there is on the inner wall of the chapel, after the cartouche of Rameses, this answering legend : " His royal spouse, who loves him, Nofre-ari, the great mother, has constructed this resting-place in the grotto of purity." Ampère, a French traveller, tells us this in his letters from Egypt, and adds, "The queen is charming, and no one wearies of meeting her likeness everywhere, and which Pharaoh never wearies of repeating." Are not they beautiful, these records of an imperishable love? They cause the dim dusky ages that separate us from the time of Rameses to vanish, and we seem to feel the heart-throbs of the man beneath the strange royal robes of the Egyptian king.

In the great ruin of the Rameseum, which a French scholar calls "an historical museum" of the reign of Rameses, near the colossus of himself was one nearly as large of his mother, Livea, with a triple crown, showing that she was the daughter, wife and mother of a king. In the same place were two statues of his mother and daughter, bequeathed to the world together, as they were associated in the love of the pharaoh.

In another temple, where huge caryatides of himself supported the pylon or entrance tower, were the statues of his fourteen daughters. Their names have come down to us, but do not sound very musical to our modern ears. By their crowns we know that five of them became queens. In all of the sculptures of his battles and marches, he is accompanied by some of his twenty-three sons. Their names are given, and they are known as princes by the royal dress, and by the braided and jewelled lock of hair which they wore during the lifetime of the king their father. By all of these touching records of the home affections we know that the wonderful baby king and boy warrior was in his manhood a tender, loving son, husband and father; and this knowledge adds a purer, brighter lustre even to his splendid fame.

That he reigned sixty-eight years is a fact so fully confirmed by data that it may be accepted as truth. Until the death of his eldest son, Sha-em-Jom, the crown prince, beloved by the people and dearest to his father's heart, the history of these long years is one undimmed by misfortune. This occurred thirteen years before his own death.

From this time the momuments give only hints of the frequent deaths of his children and of the feebleness and blindness of his last years. But it is not strange that, after eighty years of his stirring life as king and conqueror, the common lot of all should overtake even the great Rameses.

It is a pleasant finish to the old story to know that one daughter of his winter years comforted him with tender, filial love till the last of earth, and he went to his magnificent completed tomb full of years and honors. No mortal ever reached a dizzier height of fame. After more than three thousand years, in a far land unknown to his time and among a race then undreamed of, his placid, majestic face is familiar to every student. One of our most ambitious young artists could find no worthier subject for his canvas, in the last salon, than a portrait of Rameses II. Very recently I saw in our "fair city by the sea," the Thebes of our country, a magnificent mansion, the library of which was an old Egyptian hall reproduced. It abounded in lotus flowers, obelisks, sphinxes, winged globes and sacred bulls. Over the warm-hued mantel, like the red porphyry of the Nile country, was a richly framed portrait of heroic size. The gracious face, so calm and strong, the straight features, dark beard and royal head-dress of Egypt, proclaimed a strange fact. Rameses the Great, patron of libraries and learning 1400 B. C., is chosen as the guardian genius of a library in our young western capital after three thousand two hundred and seventy-seven years.

I must stop before you all grow gray and wrinkled with groping so far back through the long night of ages past. But you will not soon forget the story of the boy king of Egypt.

A CHILD IN FLORENCE.

CHAPTER I.

WE lived in that same Casa Guidi from whose windows Elizabeth Barrett Browning's poet-eyes saw what she afterward put into glowing verse. Casa Guidi is a great pile of graystone, a pile of many windows which give upon the Via Maggio and a little piazza, as the squares in Florence are called. Consequently it is lighter and brighter than are many of the houses in Florence, where the streets are narrow and the houses lofty.

According to almost universal custom, Casa Guidi was divided into half a dozen different apartments, occupied by as many families. Ours was on the second floor, on the side of the house overlooking the piazza on which stood the church of San Felice. The pleasantest room in our apartment, as I thought, was a room in which I passed many hours of an ailing childhood; a room which I christened "The Gallery," because it was long and narrow, and was hung with many cheerful pictures. It opened into a little boudoir at one end, and into the *salon* at the other. The walls of gallery and boudoir were frescoed gayly with fruits and flowers and birds.

Here the sun streamed in all through the long, mild, Florentine winters; here I would lie on my couch, and count the roses on the walls, and the birds, and the apricots, and listen to the cries in the streets; and, if a procession went by, hurry to the window and watch it pass, and stay at the window until I was tired, when I would totter back to my couch, and my day dreams, and my drawing, and my verse-making, and my attempts at studying.

I was fired with artist-ambitions at the age of ten; and what wonder, surrounded as I was by artists living and dead, and by their immortal works. It seemed to me then that one *must* put all one's impressions of sight and form into shape. But I did not develop well. Noses proved a stumbling-block, which I never overcame, to my attaining to eminence in figure-sketching.

The picture that I admired most in those days was one of Judith holding up the gory head of Holofernes, in the Pitti Gallery of Paintings. I was seized with a longing to copy it, on my return from my first visit to the Gallery. I seated myself, one evening, before a sheet of drawing-paper, and I tried and tried ; but the nose of Holofernes was too much for me. All that I could accomplish was something that resembled an enlarged interrogation mark, and recalled Chinese art, as illustrated on fans. I was disappointed, disgusted — but, above all, surprised : it was my first intimation that "to do" is not "as easy as 'tis to know what 'twere good to do."

In the midst of my futile efforts, a broad-shouldered, bearded man was announced, who having shaken hands with the grown-ups, came and seated himself beside the little girl, and her paint-box and pencils and care-worn face.

"O Mr. Hart," I cried, "do make this nose for me!"

Whereupon he made it, giving me many valuable suggestions, meanwhile, as to the effect produced by judicious shading. Still, I was discouraged. It was borne in upon me that this was not *my* branch of art.

"Mr. Hart," I said, "I think I would like to make noses *your* way."

PALACE IN FLORENCE.

"Would you? Then you shall. Come to my studio to-morrow, and you shall have some clay and a board, and try what you can do."

So the next day I insisted upon availing myself of this invitation. Mr. Hart was then elaborating his machine for taking portraits in marble, in his studio in the upper part of the city. He had always several busts on hand, excellent likenesses. His workmen would be employed in cutting out the marble, while he molded his original thought out of the plastic clay. There has always been a fascination to me in statuary. Mr. Ruskin tells us that form appealed to the old Greeks more forcibly than color. That was in the youth of the race; possibly, the first stage of art-development is an appreciation of form; in my case, I have not passed into the maturer stage yet. The rounded proportions, curves, and reality of a statue appeal to me as no painting ever did.

Nevertheless, I made no greater progress in molding than in sketching. I made my hands very sticky; I used up several pounds of clay; then I relinquished my hopes of becoming a sculptor. I found it more to my taste to follow Mr. Hart around the rooms, to chatter with the workmen, to ask innumerable questions about the "Invention."

It has been suggested that it was to this invention

of Mr. Hart's that Mrs. Browning referred when she wrote of —

"Just a shadow on a wall,"

from which could be taken —

"The measure of a man,
Which is the measure of an angel, saith
The apostle."

Mr. Hart wore the apron and the cap that sculptors affect, as a protection from the fine, white dust that the marble sheds: generally, too, an ancient dressing-gown. Costumes in Bohemia, the native land of artists, are apt to be unconventional.

It was a most wondrous thing to me to watch the brown clay take shapes and beauty under the sculptor's touch. I can still see him fashioning a wreath of grape-leaves round a Bacchante's head; the leaves would grow beneath his hand, in all the details of tendrils, stems, veinings. It seemed to me he must be so happy, to live in this world of his own creating. I hope that he was happy, the kindly man; he had the patience and the enthusiasm of the genuine artist, — a patience that had enabled him to surmount serious obstacles before he reached his present position. Like Powers and Rheinhart, he began life as a stone

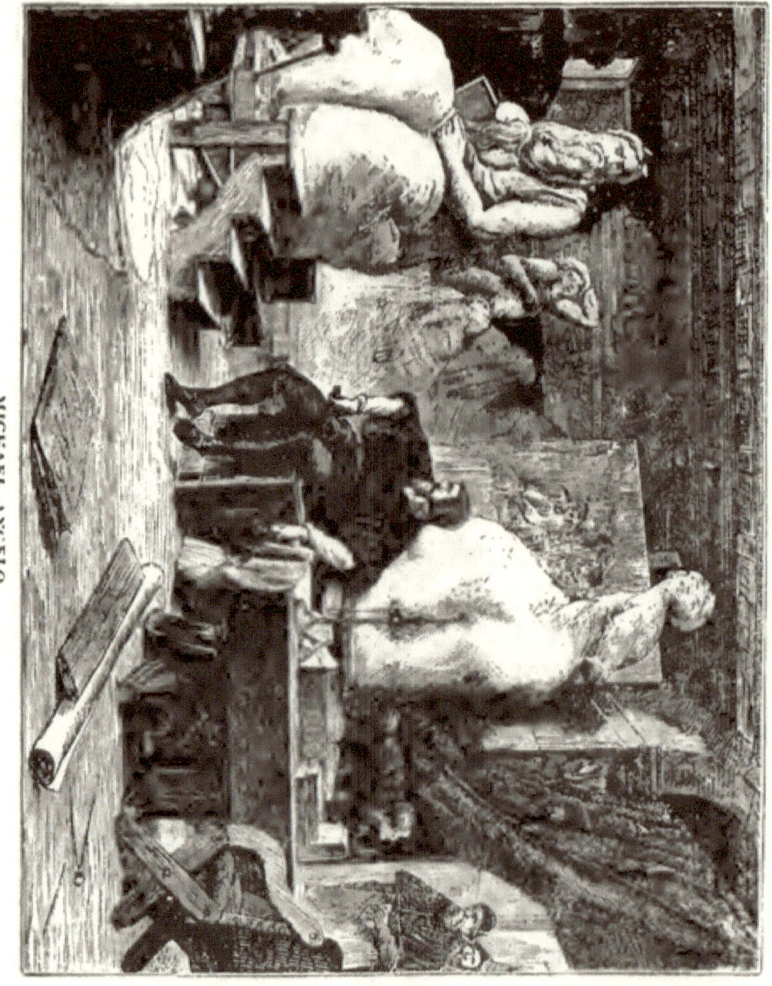

MICHAEL ANGELO.

cutter. I wonder what dreams of beauty those three men saw imprisoned in the unhewn stone, to which they longed to give shape, before Fate smiled on them, and put them in the way of doing the best that in them lay!

In spite of the fact that neither Painting nor Sculpture proved propitious, a great reverence and love of Art was born in me at this time. Possibly a love and reverence all the more intense, because Art became to me, individually, an unattainable thing. I remember passing many hours, at this period, in what would certainly have been durance vile, had I not been fired with a lofty ambition. Mr. Edwin White was sketching in a picture which called for two figures — an old man and a child. The old man was easily obtained, a beautiful professional model of advanced years; but the child was not so readily found. I was filled with secret joy when it was suggested to me that *I* should be the required model. I was enchanted when the permission was given me to perform this important service. This was before the time of the long illness to which I referred in the beginning of this paper. The spending every morning for a week or so in Mr. White's studio implied the being excused from French verbs and Italian translations. What a happy life, I thought, to be a model! I envied the beautiful old patriarch with whom I was associated in this picture. Kneeling beside him, as I was instructed to do, I thought what bliss it would be to be associated with him always, and to go about with him from studio to studio, posing for pictures.

There must be an inspiration for artists in the very air of Florence. The beautiful city is filled with memorials of the past, painted and carved by the masters passed away. I suppose that artists are constantly aroused to the wish to do great things by the sight of what these others have accomplished. Then, too, the history of the past, the religion of the past, are such realities in Florence. The artist feels called upon to interpret them, not as dead fancies, but as facts. The mythology of the Greeks and Romans meets one at every turn. I, for one, was as intimately acquainted with the family history of Venus, of Ceres, of Pallas, of Persephone, as with that of Queen Elizabeth, of Catherine de Medici, of Henrietta Maria. Nay, I was more intimate with the delightful elder set.

The heathen gods reigned sylvanly in the Boboli Gardens, and it was there that I formed a most intimate personal acquaintance with them. The Boboli Gardens are the gardens of the Pitti Palace, an immense, unlovely pile, the memorial of the ambition

POSING

of the Marquis Pitti, who reared it. He had vowed that he would build a palace large enough to hold in its court-yard the palace of his hated rival, the Marquis Strozzi. He was as good as his word; but in carrying out his designs he ruined his fortune. The vast palace, when completed, passed out of his hands into those of the Medici, then the Dukes of Florence. Afterwards it became the residence of the foreign rulers of Florence. When I remember the city, Austrian soldiers guarded the great gateway of the Pitti, and marched up and down the court-yards; and the showy white uniforms of Austrian officers were conspicuous in the ante-chambers and guard-rooms.

But behind the great palace, the fair Boboli Gardens spread away. There was a statue of Ceres crowning a terrace, up to which climbed other terraces — an amphitheatre of terraces, in truth, from a fish-pond in the centre — which commanded the city through which the Arno flowed. Many a sunny day have we children — my sisters and I — sat at the base of this statue and gossiped about Ceres, beautiful Mother Nature, and her daughter, who was stolen from her by the Dark King. Further down, on a lower slope, was a statue of Pallas, with her calm, resolute face, her helmet, her spear, her owl.

I remember that Millie and Eva and I were especially fond of this Pallas. I used to wonder why it was that men should ever have been votaries of Venus rather than of her. I have ceased to wonder at this, since then; but in those days I especially criticized a statue of Venus, after the well-known Venus of Canova, which impressed me as insipid. This statue stood hard by the severe majesty of Pallas, white against a background of oleanders and laurestines.

Then there was a second fish-pond, in the centre of which was an orange-island, about which tritons and mermen and mermaids were disposed. I can see their good-humored, gay — nay, some of them were even *leering* — faces, still. Soulless creatures these, we were well aware, and so were sorry for them. The immortal gods, of course, we credited with souls; but these — with the wood-nymphs, and bacchantes, and satyrs, that we were apt to come upon all through the garden, — these we classed as only on a level a trifle higher than that of the trees, and brooks, into which some of them had been transformed in the course of the vicissitudes of their careers.

Perhaps it is because the spirit of the old religion so took possession of me in that Italian garden, that to this day the woods, and the dells, and the rocks, seem to me to be the embodied forms of living creatures. A Daphne waves her arms from the laurel-tree; a Clytie forever turns to her sun-lover, in the sunflower.

CHAPTER II.

THE two public picture galleries of Florence — the Pitti and the Uffizi — are on either side of the Arno. They are connected by a covered way, which runs along over the roofs of houses, and crosses the jewelers' bridge, so called because upon it are built the shops of all the jewelers in town, — or so it would seem at first sight. At all events, here are nothing but jewelers' shops; small shops, such as I imagine the shops of the middle ages to have been. But in the narrow windows, and in the unostentatious show-cases, are displayed most exquisite workmanship in Florentine mosaic, in turquoise, in malakite, exquisite as to the quality of the mosaic and the character of the designs in which the earrings, brooches, bracelets, were made up. As a rule, however, the goldwork was inferior, and the settings were very apt to come apart, and the pins to break and bend, after a very short wear.

Sauntering across this bridge, one passes, on his way to the Uffizi, various shops in narrow streets, where the silks of Florentine manufacture are displayed. Such pretty silks, dear girls, and so cheap! For a mere song you may go dressed like the butterflies, in Florence, clad in bright, sheeny raiment, spun by native worms out of native mulberry leaves. Equally cheap are the cameos, and the coral, that are brought here from neighboring Naples, and the turquoises, imported directly from the Eastern market, and the mosaics, inlaid of precious stones in Florence herself.

So we come out upon the Piazza, or Square, of the Uffizi. The Uffizi Palace itself is of irregular form, and inclosed by *loggiae*, or covered colonnades. In front of the palace stands the David of Michael Angelo, in its strong beauty. Michael Angelo said of this that "the only test for a statue is the light of a public square." To this test the David has been subjected for over three hundred years, and still, in the searching light of day, stand revealed the courage and the faith and the strength of the young man who went forth to do battle with the giant, " In the name of the Lord of Hosts, the God of the armies of Israel." And who shall say to how many of us Michael Angelo does not preach, across the centuries, a sermon in stone, as we stand before his David? — as we recall what Giants of Doubt, of Passion, of Pride, we, too, are called upon to battle with in our day?

In a square portico, or *loggia*, giving upon the Piazza, is a statue of Perseus, another slayer of monsters, or, rather, a slayer of monsters in another realm. It was this Perseus to whom Pallas gave a mirror-shield of burnished brass, whom Mercury armed with an adamantine scythe, giving him also wings on his feet. It was this Perseus who slew the Gorgon Princess Medusa. In the statue, the fatal head of Medusa, with its stony stare, is held aloft by the warrior, who is trampling upon the headless trunk. This head had, in death as in life, the power of turning many men to stone, and was thus made use of by Perseus against other enemies of his. The subject of the stony-eyed Gorgon possessed, apparently, a curious fascination for artists. There is a famous head painted on wood by Leonardo da Vinci, besides this statue by Benvenuto Cellini, in the Uffizi.

How, as a child, I used to puzzle over the strange fable in both statue and picture! But, since then, I have had experience of Gorgon natures in real life; natures that chilled and repressed, stupefied all with whom they came in contact; and I wonder less at the fable, and I pass the word on to you, that you may know, when unsympathetic surroundings chill your heart and blunt your feelings, and subdue your better self, that you are being haunted by Da Vinci's very Medusa, by Gellini's very Medusa, snaky locks, fixed eyes, impassive deadness.

Into the great Uffizi Palace: up the wide marble stairway, into the long gallery that opens into the immense suite of rooms hung with pictures; the gallery hung with pictures, too, and set with statues.

How I wish I could make you see with my eyes! How I wish I could be to you something more than a mere traveler, telling what *I* have seen! That long corridor, windows on one side, statues and pictures on the other, always seems to me like a nursery for love of art. At the far end are the quaint pictures of Giotto and Cimabue. Then the reverent, religious paintings of Fra Angelico. Oh, those sweet-faced, golden-haired angels! Oh, the glimpse into the land seen by faith, inhabited by shining ones! Oh, the radiance of those pictures! The gold back-grounds, the bright faces, the happy effect of them! The artists *believed* them with all their souls, as Ruskin has said; so they painted pictures which recall the refrain of Bernard de Cluny's Rhyme of the Celestial Country. Presently pictures by Perugino, Raphael's master, and

— quite at the other end of the gallery — the portrait of Raphael, painted by himself. This picture is on an easel, and stands apart. Are you familiar with Raphael's beautiful, calm, *young* face? It is a face which has passed into a proverb for beauty and serenity. A velvet cap is pushed off the pure brow; the hair is long and waving; the eyes are large and dark and abstracted. I always stood before this picture as before a shrine.

All the way down the gallery are statues and busts. There are the Roman emperors, far more familiar to me through their counterfeit presentments than through the pages of history. Augustus, Diocletian, Trajan: to us girls they were studies in hair-dressing, if in nothing else. Some of them with flowing locks, some with close, short curls, some with hair parted in the middle and laid in long, smooth curls, like a woman. Of such was Heliogabulus, and of such was Vitellius.

One morning — soon after we came to Florence — we started off upon a quest — through the Uffizi — Millie, Eva and I, and our elders. The object of our quest was no less a goddess than she called of the Medici.

I remember that we wandered down the long gallery I have described, and through room after room. It was the fancy of our mamma, and the uncle who was

RAPHAEL.

taking care of us all, to find their way about for themselves. For instance: if we had been told that a certain picture, by a certain master, was to be found in a certain palace, we roamed in and out around the other pictures until *the* picture *revealed itself* to us. It was surprising how seldom we were deceived in this method of ours. We would pass by dozens of pictures by inferior artists, completely unmoved; then, suddenly, a thrilling vision of beauty would glow upon us, and we would acknowledge ourselves to be in a royal presence-chamber.

Such a presence-chamber is the Tribune in the Uffizi palace. We came upon many marble Venuses before we arrived in this Tribune, a large, octagon room, with a domed ceiling, blue, flecked with gold stars; but we passed them all by — until finally we entered the reverent stillness which is kept about the Venus of Venuses. We recognized her at once. There she stood, in that silent room, the light subdued to a judicious mellowness — beautiful with the fresh, smiling beauty of perpetual youth; beautiful with the same beauty that gladdened the heart of the Greek artist who carved her, hundreds of years ago; so many hundreds of years that the marble has in consequence, the rich cream-color of old ivory.

In this same Tribune hangs the portrait of a beautiful young woman, called the Fornarina. Of her only this is known, that she was the beloved of Raphael, and that she was the daughter of a baker in Rome. Fornarina means little bakeress, or, perhaps *we* should say, baker-girl. But *this* Fornarina might be a princess. An "ox-eyed Juno" princess, dark and glowing, with a serene composure about her that one remembers as her most striking characteristic.

Raphael's lady-love. Millie and I knew more about her than was ever written in books. Not reliable gossip — gossip of our own invention, but gossip that delighted our hearts.

Other pictures by Raphael hang here, too. How distinctly I recall them. How vivid are all the works of this great painter! The critics say that one who excelled in so many things, excelled also in *expression*. Yes. It is this which gives to his pictures the distinctness of photographs from life. They are dramatic. They take you at once into the spirit of the scene represented. They are full of soul, and herein lies the great difference between Raphael's works and those of other schools, the Venetian, for instance. The painters of Venice aimed at effects of color; Raphael used color only in order to express a loftier thought.

Are you tired of the Uffizi? Come with me, for a

few minutes, before we go, into the Hall of Niobe. Words fail me to relate with what mingled emotions of sympathy, distress and delight we children used to haunt this hall, and examine each sculptured form in turn. The story goes that Niobe incurred the displeasure of Diana and Apollo, who wreaked their vengeance upon the mother by killing her fourteen children. At the head of the hall stands Niobe, convulsed with grief, vainly imploring the angry brother and sister to show compassion, and at the same time protecting the youngest child, who is clinging to her. But we feel that both intercession and protection will be in vain. On the other side of the hall are her sons and daughters. Some already pierced with arrows, stiff in death; some in the attitude of flight, some staggering to the ground. It is an easy matter for the imagination to picture the supreme moment when, bereft of all her children, the mother's heart breaks, and she is turned to stone. The legend relates that that stone wept tears. Nor was it a difficult matter for me to take this on faith. What is more, many is the time I have planted myself before the very marble Niobe in the Uffizi, firmly expecting to see the tears flow down her cheeks.

So we come out upon the streets of Florence again.

Fair Florence, the narrow Arno dividing her, the purple Appennines shutting her in the Arno's fertile valley. Flower-women stop us on the streets, and

LA FORNARINA OF THE UFFIZI, AT FLORENCE.

offer us flowers. Flower-women who are not as pretty as they are wont to be at fancy-dress parties; they are apt to be heavy and mid-dle-aged, in fact, one of them, the handsomest of the band, has a scar on her face, and a tinge of romance attached to her name. It is whispered about that her lover's dagger inflicted the scar, in a fit of jealousy. Once I myself saw a look flash into her eyes, when something was said to offend her by a passer-by on the street, which suggested the idea that she might have used her dagger in return. It was the look of a tiger aroused. And after that I never quite lost sight of the smothered fire in those black eyes of hers.

I used to wonder why I saw so few pretty faces in Florence. Moreover, how lovely the American ladies always looked in contrast with the swarthy, heavy Tuscan women. As a rule, that is. Of course, there were plain Americans and handsome Tuscans; but our countrywomen certainly bear off the palm for delicacy of feature and coloring. Still, the Tuscan peasant-girls make a fine show, with their broad flats of Leghorn straw; and when they are married they are invariably adorned with strings of Roman pearls about their necks. So many rows of pearls counts for so much worldly wealth.

I stroll on, stopping to look in at the picture stores, or coming to an enraptured pause before a cellar-way piled up with rare and fragrant flowers, such as one sees seldom out of Florence — the City of Flowers.

CHAPTER III.

ONE summer we lived in a villa a short distance outside the gates of Florence. For Florence had gates in those days, and was a walled city, kept by Austrian sentinels. That was the time of the Austrian occupation. Since then, Solferino and Magenta have been fought, and the treaty of Villafranca has been signed, and now, "Italy's one, from mountain to sea!" —

> "King Victor has Italy's crown on his head,
> And his flag takes all heaven with its white, green and red."

But then the Florentines bowed their necks under a hated foreign yoke, scowling when they dared at a retreating "maledetto Tedesco" (cursed German).

The phrase "white, green and red" recalls to me the fire-balloons we used to send up from our villa garden, on the summer nights of long ago. We had, for our Italian tutor, an enthusiastic patriot, who had fought in the Italian ranks in '48, and who was looking forward to shouldering a musket soon again. It afforded him intense gratification to send the national colors floating out over Florence. Our villa was built on a hill-side, commanding a fine view of the Val d'Arno, and of the City of Flowers herself, domed, campaniled, spired. The longer the voyages made by our balloons, the higher rose the spirits of our Signor Vicenzo. He regarded these airy nothings, made by his own hands, of tissue paper and alcohol, as omens of good or ill to his beloved country.

I suppose he was a fair type of his countrymen intensely dramatic, with a native facility of expression. One notices this facility of expression among all classes. The Italians have an eloquent sign-language of their own, in which they are as proficient as in the language of spoken words. It is charming to see two neighbors communicating with each other across the street, without uttering a syllable, by the means of animated gestures. It seems a natural sequence that they should be a people of artists.

Such long rambles as my sisters and I and our maid Assunta took, starting from the villa! Assunta was the daughter of a neighboring countryman of the better sort, who cultivated a grape vineyard and an olive field, besides keeping a dairy. We had a way of happening by in the evening in time for a glass of warm milk. Assunta's mother supplied our table with milk and butter daily, moreover; butter made into tiny pats and done up daintily in grape leaves, never salted, by the way; milk put up in flasks cased in straw, such as are also used for the native wine. Was it the unfailing appetite of childhood, or was that milk and butter really superior to any I have ever tasted since? What charming breakfasts recur to me! *Semele*, as we called our baker's rolls; a golden circle of butter on its own leaf; great figs bursting with juicy sweetness; milk.

How good those figs used to taste for lunch, too, when we would pay a few *crazis* for the privilege of helping ourselves to them off the fig-trees in some *podere* (orchard, vineyard), inclosed in its own stone wall, on which scarlet poppies waved in the golden sunlight, beneath the blue, blue skies. Am I waxing descriptive and dull? Well, dear girls, I wish you could have shared those days with me. Roaming about those hill-sides, my sisters and I peopled them with the creatures of our own imaginations, as well as those of other people's imaginations, to say nothing of veritable historical characters. We read and re-read Roger's *Italy*. Do you know that enchanting book? Can you say by heart, as Millie, Eva and I could, "Ginevra," and "Luigi," and "The Brides of Venice"? I wonder if I should like that poetry now? I *loved* it then. Also, I date my knowledge of Byron to that same epoch. We children devoured the descriptions in "Childe Harold," and absorbed "The Two Foscari," which otherwise we would perhaps have never read. Byron was the poet of our fathers and mothers; but in these early days dramatic and narrative poetry was more intelligible than the mysticism of Tennyson and the Brownings, so enchanting to me now.

One evening, some friends who occupied a neighboring villa invited mamma to be present at the reading of a manuscript poem by an American poet, Buchanan Read. I was permitted to go, too, and was fully alive to the dignity of the occasion. Mr. Read was making a reputation rapidly; there was no telling what might be in store for him. The generous hand of brother artists in Florence all cheered him on his way, and accorded to him precisely that kind of sympathetic encouragement which his peculiar nature required. The group of interested, friendly faces in the *salon* at Villa Allori rises up before me as I write, on the evening when Mr. Read, occupying a central position, read aloud, in his charming, trained voice.

A Child in Florence.

I remember that, in the pauses of the reading, Mr. Powers, who was present, amused one or two children about him by drawing odd little caricatures on a stray bit of note paper, which is, by the way, still in my possession. Doubtless Mr. Powers' reputation rests upon his statues, not his caricatures; yet these particular ones have an immense value for me, dashed off with a twinkle in the artist's beautiful dark eyes.

There was also present on this occasion a beautiful young lady, for whom Mr. Read had just written some birthday verses, which he read to us, after having completed the reading of the larger manuscript. Those birthday verses have haunted me ever since, and this, although I cannot recall a word of the more ambitious poem.

Mr. Powers had lived for so many years in Florence that he was by right of that, if by no other right, the patriarch of the American colony there. He and his large family were most intensely American, in spite of their long expatriation. His was emphatically an American *home*, as completely so as though the Arno and the Appenines had been, instead, the Mississippi and the Alleghanies. This was no doubt due to the fact that Mrs. Powers was preëminently an American wife and mother, large-hearted and warm-hearted. She never forgot the household tradi-

GOING TO THE PARTY.

tions of her youth. She baked mince-pies and pumpkin-pies at Christmas and Thanksgiving, and dispensed these bounties to her countrymen with a lavish hand. Then, too, the Powers lived in a *house*, and not in an *apartment*, or, as we say, on a flat. The children ran up and down-stairs, and in and out their own yard, which lay between the dwelling-house and the studio, just as American children do. And in this genial, wholesome home an artist grew up in the second generation. A son of Mr. Powers is now making name and fame for himself in his father's profession.

It has been said that the beautiful face of the eldest daughter of this family is suggested in her father's "Greek Slave." I looked up to her then with the respect which a child feels for an elder girl, "a young lady in society." I can appreciate now and admire, even more than I did then, the extreme simplicity and unconsciousness which so well accorded with her grand, classic beauty. She was the good fairy at a Christmas Tree Festival, to which all the American girls and boys in Florence were bidden, on the twenty-fifth of December. We were all presented with most exquisitely made *bonbonnieres*, chiefly of home manufacture. We were feasted on doughnuts which brought tears to some of our eyes; dear

American doughnuts, that *might* have been fried in the land of the free. We had French candy *ad libitum;* but there was also on exhibition a pound or so of genuine American stick candy, such as we see by the bushel in this country, and which had been brought over from the United States by a friend recently arrived, at Mrs. Powers' special request. We examined this stick candy with patriotic enthusiasm. We ate little bits of it, and thought it infinitely better than our candied fruits and chocolate creams. Doubtless this little incident here recalled will account for the fact that I always associate peppermint stick candy with the flag of the Union. It is an unfortunate caprice of mind; but, nevertheless, the national stripes always rise before me when I see these red and white sticks.

I am inclined to the belief that exiles make the best patriots. We American children stood up fiercely for our own native land, whenever the question as to national superiority arose between ourselves and English, French, or Italian children, — especially the English. With these we fought the Revolutionary war all over again, hotly, if injudiciously. And I am confident that we had a personal and individual sense of superiority over them. No doubt we were endowed, even at that early age, with the proverbial national

AT THE PARTY.

conceit. Some one had told me that every American was a sovereign, and that I was consequently a princess in my own right. This became a conviction with me, and greatly increased my self-importance. How glorious to be the citizen of a country of such magnificent gifts of citizenship!

But to return to Mr. Powers. His statue of California was on exhibition at this time. This is, to my mind, the most noble and impressive of his works. The strong, resolute face, of classic outlines, and of the sterner type of beauty, bears a distinct resemblance to the sculptor's second daughter, although by no means a portrait. It has been told me that one of the fathers of our American church, traveling in Italy, suggested an important alteration in this statue. California originally carried in her hand a bar, supposed to represent a bar of solid gold. The idea occurred to the bishop that were this smooth bar — which might mean anything — made to represent a nugget of gold in the rough, the point of the story would be far more effectively told; and on this idea the bishop spoke. The sculptor was impressed directly, and with all the unaffected simplicity of real genius he thanked his critic for the hint. California now displays her symbolic nugget; and, moreover, about her head is designed a fillet of bits of ore in the rough.

A Child in Florence.

The America of Powers is another impressive and beautiful female form. A vision of the sculptor comes before my eyes, standing in front of this statue, and talking it over with a party of visitors. Such a beautiful, simple-mannered man — with his mild dark eyes and serene face! He wore the usual blouse and linen apron, and the cap of the sculptor. He held his chisel in his hand as he conversed. Some of his audience did not agree with him in the peculiar political views he held. But Mr. Powers would not argue, and what need? Had he not preached his sermon in stone, and eloquently?

CHEERFUL WORDS.*

In the whole range of English literature we can call to mind the works of no single author to which the title, "Cheerful Words," can more properly apply than to those of George Macdonald. It exactly expresses the element which permeates everything from his pen, whether sermon, essay, story or poem — an element which strengthens while it cheers, which instills new light and life into the doubting or discouraged soul, and incites i, to fresh effort.

In the volume before us the editor has brought together, with a careful and judicious hand, some of the choicest passages from Macdonald's works, written in various keys and upon various subjects, but all marked by healthy sentiment and sunshiny feeling. In quoting what a late critic has said of the "electrical consciousness" which characterizes his writings, the editor remarks: "The breadth and manliness of tone and sentiment, the deep perceptions of human nature, the originality, fancy and pathos, the fresh, out-of-door atmosphere everywhere apparent; above all, the earnest, wholesome, but always unobtrusive religious teaching that underlies all his writings, give to the works of George Macdonald a certain magnetic power that is indescribable.' And in the selections here made that power is singularly apparent. By turns they touch the heart, fire the imagination, moisten the eyes, arouse the sympathies, and bring into active exercise the better feelings and instincts of mind and heart.

The introduction to the volume is from the pen of James T. Fields, a personal friend and ardent admirer of the author. He regards Macdonald as a master of his art, and believes in holding up for admiration those like him, who have borne witness to the eternal beauty and cheerful capabilities of the universe around us, and who are lovingly reminding us, whenever they write, of the "holiness of helpfulness."

---

*Cheerful Words. By George Macdonald. Introduction by James T Fields, and Biography by Emma E. Brown. Spare Minute Series. Boston D. Lothrop & Co. Price $1.00.

www.ingramcontent.com/pod-product-compliance
Lightning Source LLC
Chambersburg PA
CBHW030315240426
43673CB00040B/1176